A Letter to the Korean American Church

A LETTER TO THE KOREAN AMERICAN CHURCH

RECONCILING THE GAP BETWEEN
FIRST AND SECOND GENERATION
KOREANS

TERENCE KIM

ANM
publishers

A LETTER TO THE KOREAN AMERICAN CHURCH

by Terence Kim

© 2019 Terence Kim and Advancing Native Missions.
All rights reserved.

No part of this publication may be reproduced or transmitted in any form or by any means, mechanical or electronic, including photocopying and recording, or by any information storage and retrieval system, without permission in writing from the author or publisher (except by a reviewer, who may quote brief passages and/or brief video clips in a review).

The scanning, uploading and distribution of this book via the Internet or via any other means without the permission of the author or publisher is illegal and punishable by law. Please purchase only authorized electronic editions, and do not participate in or encourage electronic piracy of copyrighted materials.

ISBN: 978-1-946174-11-6 Paperback

Published by:

Advancing Native Missions
P.O. Box 29 • Afton, VA 22920
www.AdvancingNativeMissions.com

Unless otherwise noted, Scripture quotations are taken from from The Holy Bible, English Standard Version, copyright © 2001 by Crossway Bibles, a publishing ministry of Good News Publishers. Used by permission. All rights reserved.

To my dearest wife Hyo-in, who encompasses the best aspects of being a Korean American Christian wife.

And to my parents who supremely did their best raising me in a foreign country.

Table of Contents

Foreword from the Author ix
Introduction xiii

Chapter 1 Real and Cultural Christianity 1
Chapter 2 The Influence of Confucianism and Buddhism 9
Chapter 3 To the Korean American Youth 19

To the Parents of Korean American Youth

Chapter 4 I Want My Children to Become… 37
Chapter 5 The Importance of Being a Genuine
                Christian Parent 51
Chapter 6 The Cost of Parenting 61

To First-Generation Korean Pastors

Chapter 7 What Is Your Vision for Your Church? 81
Chapter 8 Are We Seeking First the Kingdom of God? 95
Chapter 9 What Is the Model for Your Church? 103
Chapter 10 The Real Purpose of Youth Ministry 123

| Chapter 11 | *Encouragement for Second and Third-Generation Pastors* .... 141 |
| Chapter 12 | *The Biblical Reason for Education* .... 147 |

Concluding Thoughts 151
Special Thanks 153
The Ministry of ANM 155

Foreword from the Author

There's a reason why you picked up this book. Those key words on the cover page probably popped out to you: Korean, American, and Christian. Most likely it made you think about who you are as a person who is caught between these three worlds and is trying to figure out how to balance them all. (If possible!) You might be a frustrated youth pastor in a Korean American church, struggling to maintain honor to your leadership and obey God's Word, and these seem to clash. You may be a teenager, waiting for the day you'll get out of your parent's house and start living your own life for once.

Whatever the case may be, I pray that this book will be an encouragement for you. As someone who has been in the Korean American ministry for 10 years, it has been my constant prayer for the first and second generations within the Korean American church to unite together in peace and Christian unity, serving the Kingdom of God with the strengths and skills that it has been blessed with. The purpose of this book is to create discussion that is so desperately needed between the different generations within our churches today. I hope you will be able to relate to some of my experiences and then find encouragement and correction in scripture.

Although working toward the solution will be long and complicated, I still believe we *can* be united in love. I pray for a day when our unique culture can offer its strengths to work for the Great Commission without any hindrances. In this book, you will read many biblical thoughts on various topics. As the apostles wrote epistles to their brothers and sisters in Christ in love and for concern over their spiritual conditions, I too write this book in love for my people. As Paul wrote to many churches to correct them out of love, I too raise awareness of certain issues so that we can work together towards resolving them. If you were to ask me for my opinions on these topics a decade ago, I would have probably told you to give up, leave the Korean Church as it is and start your own. Fortunately, through correction and love from the Lord, I find ways to love my people despite their 'flaws.' Because of this, I speak the truth in love (1 Cor. 13:6) not choosing to stay silent but being bold in speaking up for what is right.

Another reason for this book is that I have a heart for the Korean American church. As a Korean myself who grew up in an America that wasn't as prepared to assimilate immigrating families as well as it can today, there were definite hurdles that Korean youth had to deal with growing up. It's been fascinating during my time in the ministry observing the changing trends and needs that exist within our churches today, but also recognizing that certain issues persist through the decades. I strongly believe that the Korean American church today holds untapped potential for carrying out the Great Commission Jesus gave us in Matthew 28:16-20. We have done so well in surviving in a new country, and making a name for ourselves in food, music, and even tv shows. It is my prayer that the strengths and skills we carry today will be used for the glory of Christ Jesus.

I pray that this book will be a blessing and encouragement for you. It was actually a blessing for me as I wrote it because of the amount of care and study required of God's Word to confirm my beliefs and concerns. In short, I hope this book will encourage discussion, prompt others to do research, and motivate some to even write their own books that offer more solutions for our churches. I hope this sparks a movement where we no longer depend on the traditions of men as the standard for how we lead our churches but let *Sola Scriptura* continue to be the standard in leading our churches today.

You picked this book up for a reason: you care. You care about the Lord, Christianity, your parents, and your culture. Deep down, regardless of our frustrations there's something within us that still cares. I do not promise or even expect minds to be changed by just one book. But I hope that it will at least promote *discussion* and *prayer*. If we were to discuss the numerous issues that exist in the church today, there wouldn't be enough pages to cover them all. However, let's seek the Lord through his word and leading of his Spirit. May the years that have gone into this book give you boldness and equip you to work toward a gospel-centered Korean American church, to bring in the glory that our Lord richly deserves.

Introduction

"Sorry, Pastor, I can't come to Bible study tonight. My mom wants me to study for the SATs."

"I can't go to the retreat because I'm grounded for my grades."

"My dad says the most important thing in life is doing well in school and making a lot of money. God isn't everything; He's supposed to help us, but we do most of the work."

If there's one thing that this generation will be known for, it will be their love for internet memes. An internet meme is usually an image with a witty caption that expresses a concept or idea. These memes have exploded in popularity as many groups of people are able to relate to a certain image and share the laughter and sometimes even pain which the image expresses. They are considered the "inside jokes" of today.

Not surprisingly, there is a particular meme that pokes fun in the Asian community known as "High Expectations of the Asian Father."

It portrays a typical Asian man with a stern expression, usually with a caption that expresses great disappointment in his children who have failed his expectations academically or financially. Its popularity among the Asian community shows how we can poke fun at the cultural stereotypes that often come within Asian families.

This kind of meme, however, can offer us insight into what is actually going on within our social groups today. It shows us that different people groups have different standards and beliefs and regardless of your stance on them, they exist.

Let me share an example:

One of the "blessings" of living in the Washington D.C. metropolitan area is that you get to experience all four seasons, sometimes within one week. When it gets cold, it is cold and when it gets hot, it's extremely hot. One particularly hot night when I was young, I decided to leave the fan on so I could sleep without melting. Shortly after I lay down, my mom burst into the room, lecturing that I should never sleep with the fan on.

Already trying not to have a heart attack from the sudden break-in, I asked my mom why I wasn't allowed to keep the fan on with this hot temperature. She simply responded, "Because you can die."

I thought she was kidding. Skip ahead a few years. One day, while checking out random articles on Wikipedia, I discovered the term, "Korean Fan Death."[1] Memories of my mom kicking the door down to my room immediately flooded my mind as I discovered the reason for her seemingly irrational behavior.

This experience, alongside many others through school and work has honed a certain maxim in my life: *Whatever we believe to be true controls the way we live.*

There will be a term I'll be repeating quite often in this book: worldview. It might be a word that you have heard in church or

---

1   Korean Fan Death – The superstitious belief that if you sleep in a closed-off area with the fan on, you will die of asphyxiation. There's even a conspiracy theory that the Korean government created this myth to reduce energy consumption during the 1970s energy crisis!

in your philosophy class. Your worldview is your current explanation of how life works, which includes your purpose in life, how you treat people, and your expectations of how things should be. For example, the person who loves money believes money will solve everything and that everything has a price. The atheist believes there is no God and ultimately man will have to determine his or her own fate. Compare this with the worldview of a Christian, who puts Jesus as the foundation of all things about life and believes we should follow everything that he taught.

Certain worldviews believe that community is extremely important, and that the needs of the many outweigh the needs of the few. Others believe the individual is the highest priority, suggesting we should spend most of our days finding our purpose, calling, and identity in life.

If you understand this concept of different people having different ideas of life, then congratulations! You're on the right path to understanding why some Korean American parents act a certain way. They are influenced by their worldviews! Just as you have desires and goals in your life that are influenced by your worldview, your parents live their lives and raise their kids based on their worldview. One of the easiest ways to discover the worldview of someone is to simply see what they love, what they spend money and time on, and how they treat other people during hardship. You'll get a general idea about what they think about life.

If you agree that what you believe to be true controls how you live, *whomever or whatever controls what you believe controls how you live.*

When we take the time to dive deeper and consider exactly where these worldviews come from, it can help us communicate better with our parents (and other people too!). Understanding where they come from allows us to speak on their level, using their terminology that they can understand and relate to. When this happens, we begin bridging lines of communication where we can begin to gently challenge their beliefs. It may seem daunting at first to try and grasp all aspects of our cultural origins, but let our love for our family members, churches, and friends help drive our work.

But before we begin, let's pause at a very important place: our own worldview.

CHAPTER 1
Real & Cultural Christianity

"He also told them a parable: 'Can a blind man lead a blind man? Will they not both fall into a pit?'"
- Luke 6:39

I don't remember the first time I went to church, but it was certainly something that came naturally in my childhood. My parents would make me go each week, so I didn't really see it as an option. Honestly, all I really remember was being bored with the praise time at various churches because the praise leader would sing 5-7 songs, repeating the chorus at least twenty times. I still remember the occasional retreats that I would go on where the guest speakers would always wait until the last day to make things utterly dramatic. They'd put us in a room with the lights off, blast Christian music at us, and scream in our faces about how God loves us.

Let's not forget the numerous times we had to go to another church member's house for the adults' Bible study. It would be an awesome night if the kid who lived there had a Nintendo and we could just play games all night, otherwise it'd be a couple of torturous hours just sitting around doing nothing.

Sometime around high school, I began to attend church less and less. When I actually went, I would get into fights with other kids at church over silly things. I became one of those people who hated church because of all the hypocrisy. Sometime in my junior year in high school, I made the decision to stop attending church entirely. I believed that I was still a Christian, that God existed, that Jesus died for my sins, and that I should follow the commandments; I just didn't see a need for going to church.

Some of you can relate to these experiences. I share mine to express how much they influence our current understanding of Christianity, the church and Christians in general. Sadly, not all of these experiences necessarily reflect what Christianity is truly about. Let's consider the fact that even though I went to church for most of my adolescence, I was not actually a Christian. I was someone who literally went to church most of my life and said and did my best to do all the "Christian things", but to be honest, I wasn't truly saved until my junior year in college. I am extremely grateful that the Lord opened my eyes, but I hope my story encourages you to reflect on your own beliefs.

There is a phenomenon that goes on in many churches today. Instead of teaching and living out what Jesus actually taught us, we have made up our own version of Christianity. This is nothing new, it has been happening since the beginning of the first church in the book of Acts. I like to call this "cultural Christianity", where we do not define our beliefs through the Bible or through what Jesus taught, but rather our own ideas, values, and yes, our culture. This concept is clearly seen within churches in many different cultures. Conservative churches can lean towards a very legalistic culture that measures your faith by how well you obey the rules which is quite the opposite of what Christ taught us. A false teaching known as the "prosperity gospel" emphasizes the fact that you can earn material wealth as long as you offer enough faith to God. In summary, cultural Christianity is one where the people, not God or his Bible, define the rules and boundaries.

The Korean church is not free from the clutches of cultural Christianity today. As many Koreans know, we are a hard-working people group who have endured suffering over the past generations. We are a proud people who strive to do our best in academics as well as our work ethic and love to show off our accomplishments in finances, our children, our homes, and our lives. You may have seen some of these behaviors within our churches as well, where we define the faith of someone by how much they serve, how many church events they attend, or even how much offering they gave last week.

Perhaps some of you have been looked down upon because of the type of clothes you wear. Others may have been hurt because they failed to meet church-goers' expectations. I can share the numerous when instead of loving those in need, people chose to gossip about them, leading to their departure.

Unfortunately, instead of doing what the church is actually called to do, many have distorted it into something that's totally not what Jesus is all about. This is one of the reasons for this book! One thing I would like to accomplish in this chapter is to clear up our current understanding and feelings toward Christianity. It will probably be difficult for some, but let's give God a chance to show us what genuine faith looks like by his word and truth. After all, we don't want to define our understanding of Christianity by our poor experiences, or by examples of people who claim to be Christian, but do not live like it.

For what it is worth, I can go on and on *and on* about my personal experiences and distaste for the Korean American church. Remember, I got into fights at churches because I hated the hypocrisy! But then I became a pastor for Korean American churches. You would think that all the hypocrisy, abuse, and conflicts that I witnessed growing up would have turned me away from the church forever. The reality is, when we actually take the time to really investigate for ourselves what true Christianity is all about, we realize God should be the frame of reference, not people.

Our experiences with different people (doctors, lawyers, English teachers, even parents) tend to mold our view of that particular profession or role. Understandably, terrible experiences often lead to negative views and sometimes even fears of certain people. My encouragement is that as we mature into adulthood, let's work toward letting go of some of these adolescent views and fears. For example, regardless of our hatred for or fear of doctors in the past, we realize that there will be times as adults where we *must* receive medical attention. Back in college, I received a speeding ticket and had to attend driving school as a result. During the lesson concerning safety and seatbelts, there was one female student who admitted that she stubbornly refused to wear them while driving. She once had a traumatic experience of her car falling into a lake and because her seatbelt would not unfasten, she was unable to free herself and escape. It's understandable that anyone who has gone through such a horrific experience would be reminded of the fear every time they fasten their seatbelts, but her one bad experience did not change the *need* for seat belts, only her *perception*. See how one terrible occurrence can influence our behaviors and beliefs?

Let's offer an example in a more spiritual context. I've been in the ministry for ten years, and as someone who grew up in the Korean church, I've had my fair share of interactions with various families and leaders. Throughout the years, I have been gossiped about, as well as lectured and yelled at for various beliefs and actions that I personally felt were biblical and godly. I have been punished and disciplined for actually doing the *right* thing. You're probably wondering if I'm crazy or perhaps a glutton for punishment? What keeps me and other pastors and leaders in my position to continue to serve the church despite the numerous hardships and pains that come with the job?

It's the fact that *Christianity is not about fulfilling an obligation, it's about responding to the love that Jesus Christ has given to us first.*[2]

Sometimes the way that Christianity is presented in the Korean American culture doesn't match up with what Christianity actually is all about. Christ gave us the standard founded in the Bible, but unfortunately, there are many who use the church to fulfill their selfish desires with totally unbiblical beliefs.[3] The reason why I bring this subject up is because I believe there are many who have been hurt by the church. Please do not let one bad experience define your perspective of Christianity. For every poor experience that I've had, God blessed me with positive experiences with authentic Christians, people who genuinely love Jesus. They're not perfect, but they genuinely follow the one who *is* perfect. The first step and challenge I have for those who have been hurt by the church as I have, is to go and investigate who Jesus really is and what he really taught.

Here are some things to reflect on as you consider where you currently stand:

- Is your faith defined by obligations and fulfillments of religious rituals? (Church attendance, retreats, bible studies, etc.) or do these things come from a love and understanding of who Jesus is?
- How did you become a Christian? Do you have a testimony? Does your testimony describe your life before and after meeting Christ?
- Is your understanding of Christianity a mere knowledge in the head or a belief in the heart?
- Do you love sharing your faith and relationship with Jesus with others?
- Would you still go to church if none of your friends went?

---

2 1 John 4:19
3 Jesus specifically warns us to watch out for these type of people in Matthew 7:15-23.

If you haven't noticed already, genuine Christianity involves a loving relationship with God, and an understanding of who Jesus Christ is. The key is Jesus! We were created by God to have a relationship with him, to enjoy and glorify him for who he is and what he has done for us. Unfortunately, because of our sin, we destroyed that relationship with him. God had every right to wipe us out and start over, but in his mercy and love, he offered a way of redemption through his son Jesus Christ. When Christ died on the cross, he took upon himself all of our sins and took the punishment on our behalf. As Christ took the punishment for our sins, he also gave us his righteousness. Whomever has faith in Christ as the only way to heaven, through his death and resurrection will no longer have condemnation but rather have eternal life with our God. This is the gospel message! Through Jesus, we not only have life and salvation, but we also have the answers to everything about life, including our origin, purpose, and destination! His resurrection gives us that hope. Being a Christian is not merely "asking Jesus to come into your heart" but rather it is an acceptance to follow Christ despite the cost. I highly encourage you to speak to your pastor, a mature Christian, or even to search YouTube to find what the gospel is, and to really see what true Christianity is all about![4]

We need to come to an understanding of genuine Christian faith for ourselves, and continue to study the origins and reasons for the Korean American church culture. When this happens, then we will be ready to work toward forgiving people and showing them what true Christianity is all about. We will go over some specific issues found within our churches today, but we cannot work toward a solution until *we* ourselves have the solution. I pray we will work toward rejecting cultural Christianity and follow Christ in spirit and truth! (John 4:24)

---

[4] Recommended Christian speakers who will clearly explain the gospel to you: John Piper, John MacArthur, Ravi Zacharias, R.C. Sproul, Francis Chan, and Timothy Keller to name a few.

Things to Consider

1. How clear and confident are you in your current beliefs? (Especially if you believe you are a Christian.) Why? If you don't know how to answer this question, does it bother you?
2. How can understanding the repercussions of cultural Christianity help us forgive and work with our elders better?
3. Who can you go to find answers to the questions that you have about Christianity?

CHAPTER 2
The Influence of Confucianism and Buddhism

> *"I appeal to you therefore, brothers, by the mercies of God, to present your bodies as a living sacrifice, holy and acceptable to God, which is your spiritual worship. Do not be conformed to this world, but be transformed by the renewal of your mind, that by testing you may discern what is the will of God, what is good and acceptable and perfect."*
> *- Romans 12:1-2*

One of my favorite times of the year as a child was New Years' Day. Despite the fact that I didn't know the reasons why nor could explain the traditions behind it, I loved the time of *sebae*. Sebae, for those who may not know, is the traditional bow that the younger generation gives to their elders in respect and for blessings for the new year. Varying from family to family, some will wear *hanboks* (traditional Korean garb) while others will eat rice cake soup (*ddukgoek*). To be honest, I was only excited because of the allowance money that I got from my grandmother after I did *sebae*.

Here's an interesting experiment we can do with our elders: ask them why we do *sebae*. Ask them for the history behind it, who started it, why we do it and why we continue to do it, and see how much they know. The purpose of this is not to show how historically illiterate they are, but to reveal how people will follow traditions without really knowing why.

Isn't it interesting to see how much this applies to so many other aspects of life? We go to public school and trust in strangers who we assume have degrees to teach us rather than our parents or other family members. Why exactly *do* we give each other presents in the Christmas season? Why must numerous turkeys have to be sacrificed to feed great multitudes of families every Thanksgiving? When we stop and think about it, there's quite a long list of things we do in life without really understanding why we do them. To reiterate, what we believe to be true controls how we live. If this is the case, let's consider that whoever controls what we believe in, controls how we live.

Enter Confucius, a well-known teacher who lived in eastern China from 551 to 479 BC. Due to repeated wars and deteriorating morals in culture, especially among leadership, he believed China was in need of a great revamping. He believed that if leadership showed certain qualities, these attributes would gradually trickle down to the culture and restore peace.

The basis of the teachings of Confucius suggested that a successful society would require relationships based on honesty and respect amongst its citizens. This had to start within the family (father to son, husband to wife, etc.) and extend outward. Every relationship in society was hierarchal and this included your friends if they were a couple of years older than you! Likewise, sons were expected to obey their fathers, young siblings were expected to respect their older brothers and sisters, and citizens were expected to honor their government leaders.

On the flip side, those who had the higher "rank" were expected to set a good example for their subordinates and use their powers wisely. They were expected to be fair and just, and be a model for those under them. Leaders weren't to be corrupt, but rather honest and leading with integrity. The same rules applied to parents who were expected to take care of their children as long as they were obedient. If those in positions of authority were immoral, they were usually shamed and hated. This gave grounds to an honor/shame structure that is well known today.

Confucius greatly believed that this system would make a society run smoothly. Ironically many of his teachings did not catch on until after his death. His followers collected his teachings into what is known as the "Analects". Roughly 200 years after his death, the Han Dynasty (one of the more well-known dynasties in China) instituted many of his teachings in their laws which still act as the basis for many beliefs held in Asia today.

Let's do a quick run-down of some of his teachings and see if you can relate them to some of the beliefs and traditions that your parents hold today:

Loyalty towards authority and *relationships* – Back in Confucius' time where kings ruled and kingdoms reigned, loyalty was an important attribute of life. First, one was to be loyal to your king, then to your family, then spouse, then friends. Loyalty was yet another gear in the clockwork of society that kept it running smoothly. Today we do not have kings so it seems that this sense of loyalty slowly transformed into loyalty to any authority figure, such as parents, pastors, and employers. Even today, many Koreans practice some type of ancestral worship, believing that even after death the elders of the family still exist in some form and hold weight in family decisions.[5] Many Korean adolescents are expected to stay loyal to their families either by providing for them by obtaining a job that pays well, honoring them through obedience, or even being influenced by them to marry a specific person.

---

5   Some may relate to this in the tradition of visiting graves, bowing to them, and drinking the deceased them by pouring alcohol onto the grave.

Confucius stressed that relationships between people were important for the running of society; that parents and elders have a responsibility to be concerned for their children. These children are taught to respect their elders, who care for them and teach them the ways of life. You may know of parents who provide for their child in almost every aspect of life possible, from providing them with a good home and plenty of food, to paying for their college tuition and even purchasing their first car. These are just some of the things parents do to show their love for their children. Ask yourselves, how many Korean parents have you seen work long hours every week just to provide a nice car for their son or daughter?

Maybe you've seen Korean adolescents show obedience and loyalty towards their parents and elders, simply submitting to all of their commands and expectations. Some give full control to parents in regard to which school they are to apply to, how they're going to spend their Friday nights, what sports and instruments that they will play, and even who they will marry! Although it is a dying tradition today, many firstborn Korean sons are actually expected to invite their parents to live with him and his wife after marriage! Confucius attributed great importance to the family structure.

Importance of carrying out roles in society – Confucius believed that people should find a role in society and practice performing that role to the best of their ability. Furthermore, no one should ever intervene in someone else's role as they aren't qualified to do so. For example, if you are a mother, you are expected to carry out certain tasks such as cooking, cleaning, and providing care for the children. These women are trained to be the best in that role, and are expected to fill that position. Many Korean wives are shunned if they are incapable of cooking, cleaning the home, or making their children behave.

Confucius also expressed the concept of the "perfect gentleman/scholar" or simply put, someone who was worth respecting and obeying. A man who carried out his teachings, gaining a position of power and financial influence, was one to be respected. Additionally, if this gentleman were to be generous and lead with integrity, especially for the sake of the community, he would be worthy of praise. If you study the history of China and Korea, you would likely notice that many of our idioms and proverbs include the names of great leaders and reflect their actions.

Perhaps the greatest impact Confucius' teachings had is found in Korean history, particularly the Joseon Dynasty which lasted for roughly 500 years, ending in 1893. One particular characteristic of this ruling government was a group called the "Yangban"[6] which consisted mainly of civil servants and military officers. These men exemplified the "scholarly official" or "perfect gentleman" that Confucius believed would be the backbone of a strong society, unlike their western counterparts, where royalty would be passed down through families.

The Joseon Dynasty allowed many people to take examinations that tested them on Confucius' teachings. If they passed, they would normally be appointed to a civil position, which would earn the respect of many. If a family was unable to produce offspring capable of meeting the requirements, they could be reduced to commoner status. Looking back, we have a better understanding of these motivations to study hard and achieve success – the same drive that many first-generation Koreans have today.

As the centuries passed, it would come as no surprise that family members would look out for each other. Within each province, the preference and priority of opened positions would go to relatives. The Yangban would even keep records of the lineage of local families to help fill open positions. Even though these were not state-legislated laws or practices, the structure was generally accepted. We still see influence of the Yangban culture in today's Korea ranging from a focus on family name, position, success, to loyalty to a certain authority.

---

6   You may have seen pictures of these Asian men in white robes, wearing circular black hats.

Sometimes big names such as Samsung[7], Korean Air[8], and others in positions of power are excused of their corruption and misbehavior. Only teachers and professors are considered capable of leading in the area of education. There is a mentality of, "he or she is considered the expert, so I will not intervene." Spiritual leaders, monks and mystics are the ones to look toward for spiritual guidance, never anyone younger or in a lower class.

How does this influence us today? Many Korean churches demonstrate a high respect for the senior pastor and his wife due to their position. On one trip to Korea, I heard of churches where the senior pastor had the final say in church decisions, even to the point where the entire church budget was under his watch! There is a belief that pastors that should deal with spiritual matters, while parents should deal with family matters like education and finances. In Korea and other Asian cultures, the school teacher is greatly respected and even given many gifts during the holidays and invited to homes for dinner. The advice from doctors is basically considered scripture to many first-generation Koreans; accepting any medicine or treatment with no questions asked. I remember on one of my trips to Korea, I was dealing with stomach issues. Although there are some over-the-counter drugs in Korea, local pharmacies are the norm. These are small drug stores usually run by one or two people. You pop in, tell them your symptoms and they give you the proper medicine. No explanations, no background checks – just pay and get your pills. At some point, you may have seen your parents react to something on the news. Whether it's a recent medical breakthrough or a new risk, they might start taking certain (sometimes unreasonable) precautions, because to question any expert is either a sign of disrespect or foolishness. It truly is amazing to see that the more we study the concepts of Confucius, the more we see the foundations of our cultural norms.

---

7   https://www.bloomberg.com/view/articles/2017-08-25/why-samsung-s-lee-needs-to-do-his-prison-time
8   https://en.wikipedia.org/wiki/Nut_rage_incident

Sometime around the fifth century, Korea received a taste of Buddhism. Though it began in India, many Chinese were influenced and as a result shared these beliefs with their oriental cousins. If Confucianism was the way of life when it came to ethics and society, then Buddhism added the religious flavor and authority behind it. Due to the structured lifestyle of hierarchy, and the roles and accompanying expectations, Koreans easily accepted the religious rituals that came from Buddhism. As Confucianism guided our relationship towards authorities, Buddhism taught us to regard leaders looked upon as guides for spiritual matters.

Let's consider these beliefs and rituals from our past, and compare them to certain habits with our Korean churches today. Senior pastors are held in high reverence, as they are the main spiritual teacher. It is often believed that a closer relationship with the spiritual guide will result in "greater blessings" as long as one follows the pastor's guidelines and teachings. The combination of the high ethical standard of Confucianism that is ingrained into our culture and the emotional and ritualistic practices of Buddhism resulted in many older Koreans holding a rigid standard in the traditions of worship and morality. An individual proves their faithfulness through obedience to the spiritual authority, as well as the amount of work and effort they put into it.

We still see fallout of Buddhist worship practices in our churches today. I point out these examples not to dismiss people's intentions, but to give a clearer understanding of their origins. Let's take the Korean style of prayer for instance. You may have seen the passion that comes during prayer time within Korean churches. Many will gather in before dawn to pray out loud for their requests. Similarly, there are eastern Buddhist styles of prayer where crying out to the heavens was common. Your commitment towards certain rites would seemingly beget more blessings.

Keep this in mind as you reflect on how Koreans define "spiritual maturity." Is it based on how many works we have performed in the church or how many offerings we have given over the years?

There are still Korean churches today that list out all the people who gave offerings the previous Sunday despite what Matthew 6:2-3 says. Many still work toward obtaining a blessing by how they treat their senior pastor. Others still define spiritual success by the attendance numbers rather than discipleship. It is worth our time to reflect on the origins of certain practices within our churches today.

By God's grace, Buddhism eventually died out in Korea as shown with the nearly-abandoned Buddhist temples of today. Due to the constant corruption of religious leaders in the past, the Koreans who were ingrained with the strong ethics of Confucianism developed a distaste for these corrupted monks and cast them out of the country. By God's sovereignty, Christian missionaries and evangelists came with the message of Jesus Christ, the one who not only held the highest moral standard, but offered hope to many in Korea who were impoverished and in great need. Christ was quickly accepted.

Unfortunately, as with most (if not all) churches, Koreans failed to completely break free from their former cultural and religious practices and habits. We may see some of these practices within our own churches today. It is eerily similar to one of the biggest issues within the early Christian church concerning what to do with the laws and commandments handed down from Moses. Were Christians to uphold their Israeli heritage and traditions such as kosher law and cleanliness? Or were they, as the apostle Paul taught, literally saved by faith alone in Christ alone? These practices were so deeply rooted into their lifestyle that it felt very strange to simply give them up!

Perhaps seeing the benefits of certain practices and rituals and transforming them in a Christian context, we too held onto some of these traditions as they were passed down through the generations. Sadly, over time and perhaps due to poor teachings, misinterpretations and hypocrisy, many of these potentially good concepts have been distorted and abused. Because the focus is upon obedience to ethical law that "proves" one's faithfulness to Christianity, the Korean American

Church has lost their love for Christ, blindly devoting themselves to mere traditions of men guised as Christianity. It should come as no surprise then, when Korean pastors become authoritarian leaders who define the faithfulness and loyalty of younger pastors and students not by their devotion to Jesus, but by their devotion to their church. This applies to many parents also; many with good intentions seeking to provide for their children in material things but failing to realize the risks of materialism and the importance of trusting in the Lord's provision.

I hope that the study of our history has given us a better understanding and a launching point towards a solution in creating dialogue within our churches today. A better understanding of the origin of certain practices can help us discern whether or not something is biblical and worth holding onto. Let's seek to follow 1 John 4 and discern all spirits, testing whether or not we are truly seeking Christ in our ministries.

Things to Consider

1. What are some celebrations or rituals you have at home or church that are done simply because it has been done that way for many years?
2. Can you reflect on some habits and practices within your church that may not be entirely biblical?
3. Do you find yourself loving and trusting more in fulfilling obligations within the church than in having a loving relationship with Jesus Christ?

CHAPTER 3
To the Korean American Youth

"But Jesus looked at them and said, 'With man this is impossible, but with God all things are possible.'"
- Matthew 19:26

Is there a solution to the problems we are facing in our churches today? The answer is an enthusiastic yes! Fair warning though, the solution is far from easy.

Some may suggest that the solution is finding the positives of both cultural beliefs and traditions and agreeing to a compromise. This may seem like a good idea, but people often clash over what is considered important, especially when the older generation is pretty rigid in their current beliefs. Others may suggest that we simply endure the issues until we're able to move out, get married, and become our own person. To be honest, the problems don't go away that easily. I have seen numerous broken families well into their adult years fighting over marriage, how to raise up children, what house to buy, or which job to get. The problems don't necessarily fade away over time.

So, as you read through the solutions offered in this book, please understand that everybody has their own unique life and calling from the Lord, which means that there is no general answer. God has given each of us different circumstances, different levels of faith, and different resources. That means we will actually have to get down to the nitty gritty and work things out based on what has been given to us.

Be encouraged! This is actually a good thing because through our unique circumstances we can receive unique blessings in many different ways. When we have to fight for the reward, it just tastes so much sweeter. Consider the numerous things that have taken time and patience to see the fruit of our labor. We may not see the results instantly, but only after a month, a year, or perhaps even a lifetime do we see the growth from our efforts. It's worth the wait! Sometimes we think certain plans are impossible from our understanding, but let's have faith that through the Lord all things are possible (Matthew 19:26).

Let's start at the beginning. We need to realize that the solution may take us out of our comfort zone. It's not really about compromising, it's more along the lines of taking medication, even if it tastes horrible. The solution isn't about choosing the right side, it's about trusting in the Lord, and working daily with what He has given us. It's bound to stretch us, and take us beyond what we consider comfortable, but that's how we grow! You may have to admit that parts of *your* own worldviews are actually wrong. It may take longer than you want it to, but the goal of restoring relationships within the Korean American community is not about what we believe is correct. It's about humbling ourselves to trust in the Lord and His ways of restoring relationships.

Although many of the solutions in this chapter pertain to our relationships to parents, I believe many of the principles can apply to relationships with the older first generation in general. As you read, pray and ask yourself, "What would obedience to this principle look like in my life?"

The Solution is Christ

One conundrum that exists is that people may know the correct answer, but that doesn't always result in following through with the correct action. Many people know that the speed limit exists, yet without hesitation, go ten miles above it with no shame or remorse. We know that smoking and drinking can lead to many different health issues, but cigarettes and alcohol continue to sell well, despite the risks.

You may have heard it before, but the main issue with today's society is the *hearts of people*.

Contrary to popular belief, people are not born innately good with a clean slate. They are born with sin. (Romans 5:12) Ever met a child who was never corrected but rather spoiled by their parents? The kid may be running around in the store screaming his or her head off, possibly even biting people[9], the parent just ignores them or shrugs it off as if nothing is wrong, or even worse, they choose to believe their screaming devil child is still their lovely angel. When's the last time you've met a child who has never been disciplined in their life and grew up to be a generous and kind person? Unfortunately, unless there is intervention and discipline, a spoiled child grows up to be a spoiled adult. As a Korean proverb says, "The thief of needles eventually becomes a thief of cows."

Let's take another example: you. Have you ever had those moments where you knew something was wrong, yet you wanted to do it anyway? Perhaps it was something that could have caused pain and disappointment, but because it was something that you believed would satisfy you and get you excited, you were willing to risk it and go through with it anyway. You know that your parents taught you that it's wrong; you can even agree with them, and you know that it's wrong! Despite this understanding, you're still struggling to stop yourself. Food, porn, wasting money, wasting time, etc.... Perhaps people have told you to hold off on dating because you're

---

9 This actually does happen more often than not.

not ready yet, but that doesn't stop you from having those desires of finding someone!

This is the sin within us. We have hearts that are corrupt and desperately wicked (Jeremiah 17:9). Without any form of intervention, we will continue to live life in selfishness. Doing good things in life or getting a proper education or a new understanding is not the solution. The Bible says the only way we can fix this problem of sin is to get a new heart that no longer desires to do what is sinful. This new doesn't lead to a perfect sinless life here on earth, but it actually wants to be obedient to God and seeks to offer genuine love towards others.

King David, after being called out for his sin of adultery and confessing his guilt before the Lord, wrote the beautiful Psalm 51: "Create in me a new heart", David prays, "and renew a steadfast spirit in me." He despised what he had done. He realized the repercussions of his sin, not just within himself, but how it impacted others. He prayed and requested not just forgiveness of his transgression, but a new heart. A new heart that would hate sin so much that he would no longer want to do those things, and a new spirit that would help him resist future temptations.

God also promises a new heart to those who will believe in him. Ezekiel 36:26 is an often-quoted verse that speaks about how God will take away our stubborn hearts which breed disobedience and give us new hearts that will seek obedience. Romans 8:9 speaks about how we are no longer of the flesh (a symbolic way of describing our selfish wants and desires that usually go against God) but one of the Spirit, one that seeks to be in tune with the will of God and his commands for us. Lastly, who can forget the well-known teaching from Jesus himself saying that we must be "born-again" to enter the Kingdom of Heaven. (John 3:3)

To put it in layman's terms, it doesn't matter how much we change the external circumstances, we must change the internal (the heart). We can share sermons, notes, and books with our parents, but if their hearts are unwilling to change, then it is all for naught. If we still suffer from pain and bitterness that makes it difficult to forgive, no matter how good the advice we receive, it will fall on deaf ears.

So with that said, here are some practical things to consider if we want to genuinely work toward restoring our relationships with our parents, our family and eventually our Korean American community.

1. We must first be right with God.

As briefly mentioned earlier, one of the traps that we can fall into is interpreting this as a first-generation or second-generation issue or an American Culture vs Korean Culture conflict. This pitfall causes us to try to find the positives of either side and somehow compromise this weird conglomeration of worldviews. The reason why this is ineffective is that your interpretation of the issue may not necessarily match or agree with another, despite your best intentions. Additionally, having the right answers in our minds doesn't necessarily mean we will do the correct thing in our hearts.

This is a spiritual matter. The heart of people reveals to us the root of the problem. We must be careful that in our pursuit for the solution, we're not just seeking fulfillment of our desires, but genuinely seeking the Lord's will for His Church.

We must first take the steps to make sure that we're on the same page with the Lord. This comes with time, knowing more about God (Hebrews 5:14) and making the necessary changes to live a life of obedience. If we are not right with God, then we make ourselves to be hypocrites by telling others how to live and what to believe in. Furthermore, if we are Biblically illiterate, how can we be confident that what we desire is actually in line with God's will?

The Christian life is not a mere shift of mentalities or beliefs, it's a transformation from no longer living for yourself to living for the will of Christ. It is a radical change that takes your entire life to grow into, so it's probably worth discussing with a pastor or a mature Christian.

You might have to take the time to answer questions such as: what is genuine faith? What's a genuine Christian? What does Christ actually say? What does Christ speak and teach about and what does that mean to you as an individual? In short, how you define your relationship with Jesus Christ gives you very good insight on where you stand in your Christian faith.

I challenge you to take the words of Jesus to heart, especially in regard to righteous judging. Let's look at the log in our eye before looking at the speck of dust in our parent's eye. The more we genuinely look at ourselves and realize we have a couple of things that we wouldn't want to discuss or confess, we realize that we're no better.

Some practical steps concerning our spiritual walk:

- ✦ Make sure your spiritual disciplines (prayer and Bible reading, attending a gospel-centered church, etc.) are healthy. I know it can be difficult when you're studying all the time. I know that sometimes after you finish your work, you want to "reward" yourself with rest and fun instead of opening up your Bible, but make an intentional decision to dedicate 15 minutes of your day to read and pray. Read your Bible in the bathroom. Listen to the Bible while driving. The issue is not about how much time we have, it's whether or not we have a desire for God. When we pray to the Lord for a desire for time to read his Word and build on our relationship with him, I guarantee that He will answer those prayers. (Psalm 37:4, Luke 11:12)
- ✦ Make sure you're spending time with mature Christian believers. We can potentially deceive ourselves in thinking that as long as we spend time with those who profess to be a Christian, then we're on the right track. Was there anything that you wanted to grow in where you did not have to push yourself? Sports? Exercise? Maybe even studying? You likely had mentors, coaches, or teachers who pushed

you to the next level. We have our excuses, don't we? "It's awkward to hang with people older than I am." "I don't know what to say." "I can't find anybody." We eventually end up spending time with people who are just as spiritually dull as we are and no sharpening happens at all. Pray and seek for a good community of believers whom you *know* will point you to Christ. A good rule of thumb is this: ask yourself, "After I spend time with this particular person, have I grown in my knowledge and/or love for Christ? Do they keep me accountable or do they just make me feel good? Are they someone worth imitating?"

✦ Reflect on your salvation and the profoundness of the gospel daily in your life. The gospel *is* worth reflecting over every single day. You will see how the good news of Christ applies to all aspects of your life, especially your relationships with others. It's nearly impossible to restore broken family relationships without understanding and experiencing the love of Christ.

2. Do not fear or hate the first generation but love them.

This is easier said than done. Especially if your parent rules with an iron fist within the house. Add other problems such as physical abuse, alcoholism and even divorce and it can seem insurmountable. I've had my fair share of issues within the family growing up, so I can sympathize with those who currently go through this right now.

What's the solution to the problems listed above? It's to love. (A reminder on why step 1 is so important!) You may remember Christ's teachings on loving our enemies. We're called to give them something to drink when they are thirsty, something to eat when they're hungry. We're called to turn the other cheek and go the extra mile for our enemies' sake. If that is the case for our relationships with those we're not fond of, then how much more shall we consider the love for our parents?

Randy Newman, author of "Bringing the Gospel Home" offers some insight into the relationships we have with our family members and loved ones. Because we have an *assumed* love for one another, we often fail to carry out the actual acts of love. Due to the lack of relational investment, we don't know each other as much as we really should, especially when it comes to our worldviews and dreams. Then we often respond in anger when they do not accept our Christian views and lifestyles.[10]

Though there are exceptions, many of our parents have grown up under worldviews explained in the previous chapter. As a result, you'll notice a lot of patterns in Korean parenting. If we agree that we hold certain worldviews today molded by our past, isn't it the same for our parents? Do you want to gain sympathy for your parents? Simply ask them about their past struggles, their experiences when they were young, and perhaps even their relationship with their parents as they were growing up. As you get the chance to learn more about them, you realize they need just as much love as you do! When we love someone who has hurt us, we are trusting that the Lord will work and speak in that person's heart.[11]

Reflection time: Think about a time where you were frustrated, saddened, and depressed over something. Deep down, you wanted people to hear you – listen to you, even just comfort you with a hug. Let's be real, within your frustrations, you vented, expressed more frustration, and mistreated others due to your bad mood.

One of the biggest keys to loving your difficult parent is understanding that they too are a person, a sinner who is in need of grace. I believe in both the nature and the nurture school of thought, that your birth, as well as your environment influences what type of person you will become. When we understand our fallenness due to sin, and the

---

10 *Bringing the Gospel Home*, Randy Newman ISBN-13: 978-1-4335-1371-8
11 This author shares this with one caution: If you or your family members are in physical danger, do not, *do not* hesitate to get outside help and tell someone. Do *not* tolerate physical, emotional, and verbal abuse. You *can* do something about it.

broken beauty of creation, as well as the ongoing sin in the world waging war against our beliefs and hearts, we realize that our parents are struggling with the same issues.

I strongly believe that the Lord helps us in understanding our parents when we seek insight into their past. As kids, we believe our parents are immortal invincible beings. There's nothing unnatural about that, but as we grow up and mature, let's remember that just as we have many issues in learning how to "adult", our parents too are still learning how to deal with this life.

Let common struggles serve as a conversation point! Ask them about their childhood and their struggles. Some of you guys may have heard your parents say stuff about how much they struggled when they were a kid. It's not uncommon to hear "you guys have it so good now!" This may just be a window into the hardships that they have gone through in their youth.

Just as our emotions are stirred whenever we see those starving children overseas, let us too have a heart of love for our parents, who also have gone through hardships in their lives which have influenced them to become the people they are today.

3. Do not be afraid to gently challenge them with the Word of God.

One of the greatest privileges that I have today is friendships with people who are parents. I have the honor of enjoying a relationship with their family, which includes their children, and they share with me their experiences of parenthood. Although I have read and heard this so many times, until I have children of my own, I probably won't truly appreciate the fact that kids do a good job in pointing out the sin in your life.

That's a great thing though! How amazing is it that God uses these young ones to be so frank in calling a spade a spade and showing us our mistakes? Some prideful parents will try to hide it through anger and an authoritarian parenting style, but I bet deep down, even they experience regret and shame in their hearts. This is not a call for youth to literally challenge everything their parents say (no matter how unbiblical it is) as that plan isn't really going to be effective. Remember, we want a gentle approach, allowing the Lord to speak to their hearts through his Word and Spirit.

We've already gone over the importance of loving God first and then loving your parents. One of the best ways to honor our parents and the Lord at the same time is through obedience. When it comes to Korean Parents: *Disobedience breaks communication. Obedience helps communication.*

Now, we know it's not that simple. What happens when our parents tell us to do something that seems to clash with God's Word? What do we do when they say you can't go to Friday night Bible study, because it's not worth your time and you need to study for your SATs? This is where the prayer aspect comes into play – where you will really need the leading of the Spirit to give you guidance on how to respond (and also how to respond gently in the heat of the moment!) I hesitate to give generalized advice here, as it is one of those case-by-case scenarios, but I do encourage you as you read through the rest of this book to discover some discussion points. The more we know, the better we can communicate with and understand our parents!

I encourage you guys to do your best in respecting the wishes of your parents, and let that offer more leverage when you take the time to communicate with them. 1 Peter actually speaks about the benefits of suffering and still offering a pure testimony despite being mistreated. In our response of love and willingness to do what is right, we send a bigger message to those who mistreat us. It really is difficult to argue against love!

4. **Take initiative in your responsibilities and show your parents that you are taking charge of your life.**

Imagine this scenario with me for a second: You are a straight-A student with a couple of extracurricular activities under your belt. You make it a habit to study and finish your work first and then do something "smart" during your free time such as reading. Every time your parents walk into your room, you're basically doing something that they approve of.

Now consider the opposite, someone who doesn't really have these qualities and habits. They have to be constantly pushed into and told to do even basic responsibilities. They don't help around the house. They tend to just mooch off of people and are very passive in discovering what they would like to become.

If you were a parent, which one would you give more leeway and freedom to?

Don't get me wrong, I'm not advising you all to become people pleasers, nor am I claiming that the expectations of your parents are always 100% correct. I just want you to take into consideration that the weight of your words are measured by your lifestyle. We like to excuse ourselves by saying things like, "I never learned this" or "They don't teach this in school" and then excuse ourselves from adulthood, but this is not the right response. Peter also speaks about this in his first epistle to Christians who were being persecuted for their faith. "What good is it, if you get punished for sin? But if you do good and suffer, this is a gracious thing in the sight of God" (1 Peter 2:20).

In short, if you know in your heart that something is wrong and yet do nothing to strive to fix it, you're just whining. If it truly was something important to you, wouldn't you put in that effort? Sadly, this is part of the culture that we live in today, where we gladly promote movements because it makes us feel like we're supportive of a great cause. When it comes at no cost, of *course* we would 'fight' for justice! However, the true test of authenticity is how much pain and suffering we are willing to go through to achieve our goals.

I strongly believe that this whole issue between the first and second generation of Korean Americans is still solvable in the name of Christ. It's just that many of us are unwilling to pay the price to achieve this goal. Let me make it clear: step up, be committed, find mentoring, and do what it takes. This *is* achievable if you're willing to put the effort into it. For those who are legitimately clueless on where to begin, I have great news for you! There are plenty of people out there who are willing to teach and mentor you to help put you on the right track. It's a matter of whether or not you're humble enough to learn and committed enough to keep learning. Sometimes the reason we don't have an answer is because we run away from the correct one.

Both sides can either continue in their pride and claim they hold no wrong, or they can humble themselves and be willing to begin that work to promote conversation. If I can encourage you by stating that there IS an answer to this issue, would you be willing to work toward resolving that issue?

Some Final Things to Reflect On

There are probably numerous examples of issues that exist among kids and their parents, but here are some practical things to consider and a few things you could say to promote discussion with your parents. You can do it! Just be confident! Trust in the Lord and he will give you the strength and boldness to stand firm for truth!

1. **Remember that our parents are imperfect, but most still have the best intentions for you.**

    Parenting is hard! Don't believe me? Just search for books on raising children on Amazon. Look at the exasperated faces of couples with a newborn. Parents will make mistakes. Sometimes these mistakes come from improper worldviews, sometimes they come from previous hurts that they hold, and sometimes just poor advice. Regardless of your situation, keep in mind that they are the parents whom our Lord has given you and who actually do try their best in raising you. The more we realize that we're all in the same boat, the easier it will be to love them back!

What if we viewed some of their methods with positive intentions? For example, many within the Korean community have parents who obsess over academics. Many believe strong grades will give you more opportunities later on (they do) and will offer you a better life, quite possibly a better life that THEY did not have. Why do they forbid you from going to many "fun activities?" Because there *are* many hidden dangers in the world that as teenager we don't recognize. Why won't you buy that one thing that all your friends have? Perhaps because they've also had many things they desired and realized it was a waste of money because of how temporary it was. As you discover their intentions, seek to partner with them in discussing biblical principals concerning how we should actually live in respect to certain aspects of life. If you haven't noticed already, see the importance of being biblically equipped to be able have these discussions?

2. If your parent commands you to do something that goes against God's Word...

This is one of those "shouldn't be answered with a generalized answer" issues, but I will share some thoughts:

Draw the line at sin. It's very unfortunate that there are parents who prevent their kids from coming out to Christian events and this should be reviewed in a case by case basis. In general, for the sake of peace, consider honoring their wishes as you ultimately honor the Lord. (Ephesians 6:5-8) As we discussed earlier, your good behavior gives you a better testimony. Consider Paul's relationships with the soldiers when he was in jail; consider how wives are to treat their unbelieving husbands (1 Peter 3). Consider how Christians are to respond to government authority (Romans 13). Missing a Bible study isn't a "sin", although sadly it does impact your spiritual discipline and community life. Challenge your parents gently and lovingly, "I wish to honor you and I will do what you want me to do, but isn't God important too?"

"Isn't eternity important as well?" Ask questions that allow the Lord to challenge their hearts.

To be clear, definitely draw the line at sin. If your parents promote behavior that is sinful and harms others (stealing, drunkenness, adultery, etc.) then you're under no obligation to follow them as you are first called to serve the Lord.

3. Communicate with your parents outside of arguments

Here's a reality that Koreans don't like to admit: they hate confrontation. Because of this fact, they would rather keep issues to themselves or gossip about it with someone else. Unfortunately, this means usually the only time they actually *do* communicate issues is within heated arguments. When emotions are high, hurtful comments that neither side actually mean to say are common. I encourage readers to communicate during times of peace as much as possible. Sitting down with your parents to share your heart, promoting a partnership rather than, "I want things done this way." Work peaceably towards being a family that honors the Lord. How effective is it to share the gospel within an argument? Not so much. Pray for opportunities to speak up during times of peace to communicate with a sober mind.

Oh, and by the way, don't give up just because your parents didn't listen the first time, the third time, or when they forget over time. When's the last time you changed your behavior in one day? When we continue to *consistently* show love first, you may be surprised that cracks appear in even the hardest of hearts!

There are so many other unique cases and examples within families today, but I hope these give you both encouragement and guidelines to help restore relationships and bring peace into a Korean household. If you already forgot, remember to work on yourself first! Your relationship with the Lord and understanding his love first is key. Remember to find a good community of strong (authentic) Christian believers who can encourage you and love on you when the going gets tough. Continue to pray for the hearts of your entire family (yourself included) as you seek the Lord. The ultimate goal is not to have a perfect family that satisfies your desires and wants, but a family that loves Jesus Christ so much that they can't help but love one another.

Want to hear something encouraging? When you actually take the steps to invest in restoring a relationship with your parents, you find yourself loving them more. Let's remember that they're still our parents, and we are their children. There are long-term benefits in their standards that we may not be able to see until much later. Our parents know our habits, and things that are good for us, and observe things in life that we do not understand now. There is a reason why Paul tells kids to honor and obey their parents in Ephesians 6. It comes with a promise! When we honor those who have good intentions for our well-being, we will reap the benefits of a long life.

Love Christ, know who you are, and seek to love your parents.

Things to Consider

1. How would you define your current relationship with Jesus Christ?
2. List three things that you would like to discuss with your parents. Write down the end result that you would like to come from those discussions. Now, find biblical support for your desires. Can you find any? If not, what does that say about your desires?
3. Who is someone in your life that can help encourage and mentor you in speaking with your parents?

To the Parents of Korean American Youth

CHAPTER 4
"I Want My Children to Become..."

"Fathers, do not provoke your children to anger, but bring them up in the discipline and instruction of the Lord" – Ephesians 6:4

Parenting is hard.
Sometimes we have the absolute best intentions for our kids, but they still end up going down the wrong path.

Sometimes we offer them the best, and they return with nothing but ungratefulness.

Even worse, some will end up at the police station in tears, wondering what we did wrong, and worrying about what to do next.

I've worked with youth for about ten years, both academically and pastorally. In all that time, I've seen plenty of families with joys. I've had the privilege of working besides parents who love the Lord and truly want their child to grow in His ways. On the flip side, I have also seen families with problems. I've had difficult experiences with parents who were at best, missing, and at worst, abusive.

With that said, let me be absolutely clear: we love you. We, meaning people who recognize that something is not right, people who see the pain and hurt that is found in any broken relationships amongst families.

I write this to the wife who holds the burden to take care of your children and their emotional, physical, and spiritual needs, but to balance a relationship or conflict with your abusive spouse at the same time. I write this to the father who bears the burden of being strong, providing for your children, sometimes hiding the fears and emotions you experience raising your child. I want to encourage those who read this that there are answers, solutions, and help for the issues at hand. Whether it is your own children, your spouse, or even issues within yourself, the answer is found in Christ, in his truth, and his love.

We need to first ask ourselves a difficult question: Are we willing to let go of certain pieces of our identity that come from our culture, history, and beliefs? This is easier to consider when it feels like there's nothing left to lose, but I encourage and plead with you to stop and reflect on the long-term effects that your current parenting style has on your child. In this instant-gratification society that we live in, we are not used to investing in long-term plans or considering possible hidden ramifications of today's choices. This is especially true concerning the way that we raise up our youth today. I pray that the solutions and encouragements offered in this book are not just used to flee from current hardships, but to genuinely seek long-lasting effects that will promote genuine love in our relationships.

There are two major questions that Korean parents should be asking themselves as they raise up their children: What is my greatest desire for my child and why do I trust that that method and philosophy is the correct one?

You can tell a lot about a person by listening to their dreams and desires (Matthew 6:21). Anyone who has ever been in ministry in any sense will understand when I say, you don't even have to hear them speak, for their actions speak louder than words. Popular Christian speaker and teacher Timothy Keller once said, "Our idols are found within our nightmares." Simply put, whatever brings stress or fear or defines our "bad days" gives us very good insight into the things that we truly do care about. For the boy who idolizes his relationship with his girlfriend, you will see an unhealthy fear of breaking up. For the little child who idolizes video games, take away the controllers one day and see the reaction. For Korean parents, look at their reactions when their child tells them that they want to become a pastor or missionary someday.

Even though we are adults, we too have our idols and sometimes it can be our *own children* (their happiness, their successes, their academics, their marriages, etc.). This can often be reflected through our constant scrutiny over their behavior and accomplishments. We may have an unhealthy obsession over their failures and mistakes and disguise it as "concern." Then comes the day when they begin to rebel and go against what seemed to work for many years. Suddenly, they show strong aggression against you and your rules over them. Maybe they want to change churches, or stop going to church entirely, or maybe they develop an addiction that you worked so hard to protect them against.

Ever questioned why these types of things happen? Even when it felt like what you did was so right?

Let's begin investigating the foundation of the solution.

What is Your Worldview?

Earlier in this book, we discussed the origins of our culture and the beliefs and traditions that come with it. We, as hard working, intelligent Koreans, have done a very good job in passing down these practices and beliefs. These beliefs and traditions are held so strongly, sometimes corporal punishment is used on those who do not follow our ways. We hold loyalty and diligence in high regard, which are shown through our successes and growth in our motherland. There are numerous examples of Korean families migrating to America with nothing, yet within a few years, they own a home, own their own business, and have sent their kids off to ivy league schools.

Have you ever stopped to reflect on origins and reasons behind our Korean culture and lifestyle? Why is it that many older generation adults have a tendency to lean towards success for themselves, as well as their own kids? I do not deny that our experiences growing up have molded our current beliefs. There are many who live in poverty and do their best to overcome these odds to live a life without hardship. Many of us who grew up this way do not want the same for our families, so we work the long and difficult hours to provide the best for our children.

Despite our best efforts and intentions, things just don't always seem to work correctly. Even though we offer the best homes, cars and food for our children, it seems like they become increasingly ungrateful. Even though we offer them a life of safety, where they can simply study freely without any difficulties that we suffered growing up, they seem to waste it away doing nothing at home. Amidst all these things, they even have the audacity to tell you that *you* don't understand, you don't care for them, or you don't love them at all, *despite* all the things that you have given them! What is going on?

Multiple times through my years in ministry, I have had parents come up to me, pleading that I speak to their child to encourage them to come out to church on Sundays, to stop doing drugs, or even to do their homework. I've seen parents blame youth pastors for "not doing their job" because their own child (in a large youth group by the way) was *failing school*. Likewise, I can't even tell you how many students have I've seen grow up never seeking advice from their own parents. They instead choose to hear the words of their peers, who deal with the same issues. I wonder what percentage of church-attending youth today in the Korean American church are still unwilling to pray or discuss spiritual matters with their own parents because it's awkward. How many more complaints of students will youth pastors today have to listen to about their moms and dads because it's so difficult for them to feel heard and treated as a human being?

What is the reason for this significant gap of communication? Our Korean mentalities demand utmost loyalty and respect which leaves no room for questioning or discussion. Should we honestly be surprised when our own children begin to cut us off from their lives? Some may argue, this was the way that they were brought up, but the question then is, why do you believe that way is the correct way? This goes back to the question of, where do our current worldviews come from and why do we trust that to be the correct way? This is the first step that we must take: *We must assess where our current worldviews originate from, such as our stances on how to raise up our children, how to discipline them, how to serve in our marriage, whether or not to go to church, and how to run a business.* The way that we treat these responsibilities stem from your current worldview.

If you want an explanation over the origins of our heritage, head over to chapter 2, where we investigate the influence of Confucianism and Buddhism over our culture. Right now, let's take two major worldviews that make up the majority of the Korean culture today and see their limitations. Again, please understand that this is not a call to throw away these worldviews completely, but merely presenting the reality that perhaps your current one cannot solve every issue!

Deception 1: Academics is Life

"I said in my heart, 'I have acquired great wisdom, surpassing all who were over Jerusalem before me, and my heart has had great experience of wisdom and knowledge.' And I applied my heart to know wisdom and to know madness and folly. I perceived that this also is but a striving after wind. For in much wisdom is much vexation, and he who increases knowledge increases sorrow." – Ecclesiastes 1:16-18

Consider the life of Christopher Langan.

For those who may not know, he is considered one of the smartest people on the face of the earth. His intelligence quotient is suspected to be in the 190-210 range.[12] In his spare time, he seeks to come up with his own scientific theories that this author wouldn't attempt to describe for fear of embarrassing himself. Chris was one of those people who found school boring. He took a nap during his SATs and received a perfect score. He also had a reputation of correcting his professors in college because he felt he could teach them, rather than the other way around. On January 25, 2008, he appeared on the trivia show "1 vs 100" in which he won a grand total of $250,000. He used this money to retire and purchase a horse ranch with his wife, much to the dismay of many who opined his mind was being wasted, as they believed he would have been capable of solving many great things.

The question arose: why would such a smart and capable man have no drive in using his skills to contribute to something worthwhile? It would not be surprising if a man of his capability could find a cure to a serious disease or perhaps even solve the problem of world hunger.

There is one prominent reason: Chris never had a solid mentor in his life.

Unfortunately, Chris had a difficult childhood. Going through four fathers, the last one being abusive, Chris never really had a person to look up to. He never had a mentor, someone who could help guide his paths, to apply his knowledge to real life, and perhaps even use his skills to help others. Here was a man who was perfectly capable of being accepted into the most prestigious universities in the country on full scholarship and yet chose to attend minor colleges, at his own expense, and then eventually walked away from the world of higher academics entirely.

---

12 IQ does not seek to measure how much knowledge a person has (although that certainly contributes to it) but rather how well one is able to apply that knowledge and solve problems in real life. The average IQ is 100, while most college students have an IQ of 120. College does not increase one's IQ, but rather those with above-average IQs tend to attend higher-level learning.

I share this story about Mr. Langan not to insult him, but simply to use him as an example to point out one of the biggest and ongoing issues within the Korean culture today: the idolization of academics. Sure, we like the positive stereotypes that come from our obsession, "Those Koreans are so good at mathematics!", "I wish I were as smart as you Asians!" Yes, as a teacher myself for five years, I've seen many Asian students fulfill those stereotypes with their long hours of study in order to strive for academic excellence. Unfortunately, within our churches there seems to be little to no discussion over the negative impacts of a high focus on academics. In fact, I would go so far as to say that many Korean families today probably know it is an issue, but either choose to accept it as it is, or have no idea how to fix the issue at all.

This is the reality, as shown through Chris Langan: intelligence alone is insufficient when it comes to living life, especially when we are not taught practical ways to apply that knowledge. Sometimes we separate this into, "book smarts" and "street smarts." Book smarts covers facts and knowledge that we often learn within the classroom while street smarts means people are capable of adapting and surviving within the environment and circumstances they're in.

I'll share a story of a student I once worked with whom, I'll call "Randy" for the sake of privacy. Randy was a very intelligent person. The math that he was taking in high school was the math I struggled with *in college*. He attended a high school where an assessment test was required and only had a 16% acceptance rate. Within this school, he graduated with a GPA that I had didn't even realize you could attain without cheating.

However, once Randy left home to go to college, he fell into a crowd known to drink often, party whenever there was free time and even be promiscuous with women. Sadly, as his youth pastor, I observed on social media slow descent of the quality of his life. The drinking and partying became more frequent and his grades suffered greatly to the point of academic suspension. His parents were obviously heartbroken and disappointed, wondering what happened to their academically strong son. This was unfortunately not the only case like this I had to deal with in the ministry.

"Bobby" was another incredibly intelligent and gifted individual. I've had the privilege of serving with him within missions trips for many years. Once he set off for college, he had a plethora of opportunities and invitations from organizations for internships. I proudly wrote a letter of recommendation for him and he accepted a position from an organization that I was close with. A few weeks later, I received a phone call from the director who wanted to talk about Bobby. He expressed that he was incredibly qualified and intelligent and did his work well, however he had major issues with working with other people. Bobby spoke to others in a condescending way, arrogantly boasting how "easy" it was for him. It was definitely a shock to me as I reflected over the director's words and realized that I never actually observed him working with others "beneath his level." His years in school alongside other intelligent and capable students never gave him the experience to be humble and kind to those who needed to be taught. Not only that, I realized later that because of the highly competitive environments of his schools, he viewed others not so much as colleagues, but opponents.

There is nothing inherently sinful in desiring great academic accomplishments, but do you see some of the hidden repercussions when it becomes our greatest cause? Many Koreans believe this deception that the academics alone, the degree alone, the name of the school alone is our main responsibility when it comes to parenting our children, but as we have seen through the story of Chris Langan, Randy, and Bobby, this is not the case. We need to ask ourselves the question: Would we consider it a success if our child became that doctor, or lawyer, or wealthy businessman, or whatever we wanted them to turn out to be, even if it came at the cost of their moral compass and ethics? Would we be fine with our children becoming a doctor with multiple marriages? Would we be fine with a son who works long hours throughout the week to honestly offer the best things of the world to their family, but never actually spent time with them? Would we be happy and satisfied if our children were academically and financially successful, if it came at the cost of a healthy relationship with you?

The responsibility of raising our children includes not only their scholarly aptitude, but who they are as a whole. Their social skills, their moral cognition, their passion and their drives – we must be honest with ourselves and ask whether or not we are doing a good job in raising up all, not some, of these attributes.

Deception 2: Children Must Uphold Our Heritage

If you have taken the time to look through Chapter 2, and see the origins of our beliefs and where some of our practices stem from[13], you may now have a better understanding of why conflict occurs. Due to different time periods, environments, circumstances, and cultures, we have various worldviews clashing between the young and old, traditional and contemporary, as well as those from the East and the West.

One of the key things that we need to understand (and accept) is that even though we have Korean children with Korean blood, they are growing up in a western culture with western ideals. It is possible that your rules and standards will work at home because they are under your roof, but can you say the same when they are faced with western issues at school? What about when they interact with people with American values or when they work for a boss who has no knowledge or desire to cater to the cultural needs of an Asian? This is the reality that a lot of our children face as they grow up here in the US. We may have loving intentions in raising them up to remember their identity as a Korean, but if done incorrectly, they can be torn between the western demands of their host country anmd the eastern demands of their parents. I would like to be clear. This is not a call for us to give up our cultural identity

---

[13] Chapter 2

nor to replace it by becoming American, but to simply take the time to reflect on whether or not there is a better method. This can be difficult to accept, especially for those of us who have been brought up being taught the importance of loyalty to our families and our cultures. It feels treasonous to even consider anything that's non-Korean.

This is the struggle that I challenge Korean parents living in America to consider, especially for those who genuinely want a family that *will* love one another, a family that seeks children with character and integrity, as well as the smarts. Will we continue to trust in a system that a growing number of youth despise and are waiting for the day to walk away from, or will we try a better way? A way that does not ask us to throw away our cultural identity, but simply asks us to place it secondary to what's actually important, our identity in Christ. God calls for us to deny ourselves (Matthew 16:24) which includes our desires, our life goals, and what we identify ourselves with, including our culture! As stated in the beginning of this book, the goal here is not to pick and choose bits and pieces of the American and Korean cultures nor is it to simply give up one and embrace the other, but it is to understand that what we may have set aside as a secondary or tertiary priority in our lives might have actually been the answer we've been looking for all along.

The Actual Problem: The Condition of Their Hearts

We have taken the time to investigate how our culture and academics cannot fully explain nor solve the problems found in mankind. Sure, there is definite overlap in how cultures explain certain behaviors and traditions. (Italians love to be loud when they speak, or Japanese focus on respect, etc.), but they do not cover the bigger questions that people ask about life, such as the origins of man, the purpose of life, and our destination when we die. Culture, at most, is descriptive of the problems we have in life, but it can never be the solution to the main issue: sin. We can have all the right laws and practices in the world, but when the hearts of people are unwilling to do what is actually right, then failure is inevitable.

Therefore, we cannot give a blanket description of the issues within the Korean church as a "Korean problem", nor is it simply a youth problem. It is a **heart** problem. A heart problem that can only be changed through Jesus Christ (Romans 7:14-25). The reality is this, the reason why our youth act the way they do is because of the condition of their hearts and the same thing applies to us!

This is the cause of the unfortunate common occurrence of youth seemingly making a drastic change in personality. Think about kids who seem so well-behaved in their adolescence, but after receiving a taste of freedom (often known as college) the rebellion exponentially grows. Things that we have tried so hard to protect them from, such as drugs and alcohol, are now part of their weekly lives. Even though we may prune off some misbehavior through discipline and punishment, if the heart of the person still desires those things, the minute that a chance appears, they will take it to satisfy themselves! This was a common occurrence among many graduating high schoolers, and perhaps even prevalent among girls growing up in oppressive environments. I would say a good majority of female students that I have worked with have had strong desires to go to school out-of-state or at least "far away" to get away from their home environment. The main reason? Because they want to "find themselves." Because they have been told what to do for so long in their youth and had no freedom to discover things on their own, they desperately want to leave that environment to try out new things that they were forbidden from doing for so long! Many, after tasting this freedom of "adulthood" will come back home during academic breaks and old conflicts and differences becomes more heated. They want to cling to their new identity which gives them so much more freedom.

I can share many more stories of conflicts that the youth have had with their parents. Whether it's a student who brings a non-Korean home and tells them that they're dating, or a student who has made a life decision that didn't match the desires of the parents. These things have one thing in common: the actions and decisions of these students come from the condition of their hearts. We need to understand that good intentions alone in raising our children are insufficient. What we believe to be "good behavior" can actually just be temporary behavior modification and because the heart of the youth is unchanged, the minute that they have the freedom to seek out their desires, many will do so!

Let's take the time to reflect on some questions: Am I raising my child to have the right heart that leads to proper behavior, or am I simply promoting behavior modification where they obey (for now) what I tell them to do, but never touch upon the root of their desires? Does it seem like I just punish them to stop the behavior so that I can get temporary relief? Or am I truly striking at the root cause of the issue?

I've had the privilege of working with a variety of people of various ages and issues, ranging from marital, to drugs and alcohol, addictions, and mental illnesses. Although I'm not a professional, one thing that I've learned to appreciate is the effectiveness of biblical counseling. Biblical counseling is not simply psychological help by a professional who happens to be Christian, but rather it seeks to determine the **root cause of the problem: the desires of the heart**, explained through biblical truth. The end goal is working toward seeing Christ as the solution to the issue. Sadly, today many easily resort to medicine or extreme methods of punishment and discipline (such as military school and constant guilt-tripping and shaming) without really trying to discover the root cause of the issue. Sometimes we can try to excuse behavior simply by saying that the adolescent is "going through a phase" or "all teenagers act like this." I am not dismissing those possibilities, but I am warning that we should stop looking for general and broad solutions to our children's behavior and begin treating them as unique individuals whom God has given to us to take care of. *Let's try to stop changing the external all the time and really seek to transform the internal.*

Another question we should consider: Do we want Christian children or just well-behaved children?

At a quick glance, it seems like those two things should be one in the same, but we need to remember that the behaviors of all people, including our kids, stem from the heart. Just as we are good at hiding, distorting, and spinning the truth for our advantage, many youth today are just as capable of simply hiding their true intentions until they finally have the freedom to carry out their desires.

It is imperative that we reflect on how we raise our kids. We have to understand that there are certain disciplinary methods that may fix the current behavior temporarily but do nothing to attack the root of the problem. An issue of a teenager who habitually ignores a curfew is more than just a matter of poor manners and disobedience. There might be something that he desires or believes in his heart that causes him to dishonor the agreed time. A daughter who continuously finds new dating partners to spend time with outside of the home may actually be searching for genuine love and value that should have been given to her from a father figure.

I still remember a student, "Esau" that I worked with who had an issue with smoking marijuana. His parents requested that I have a one-on-one discussion with him. There was probably something deep down that was causing him to do these things. Fortunately, he opened up. Part of the reason was because he was so stressed from his home environment concerning academic pressures from his parents, and smoking pot with his friends was one of the few ways he could decompress from all the stress. Although the academic expectations of parents don't apply to all circumstances, it is something for us to examine when it feels like no amount of words change the behaviors of our children. Let's remember the fact that we as Koreans sometimes resort to simply lecturing our kids, reminding them of what they have been "blessed with" and how easy they have it today. The reason why this isn't always effective is that in the perception of the youth, they don't want to be compared; they preferred to be heard. The challenge comes in working with kids as they *are* still young and at times genuinely do not know what they're doing. However, when considering our intentions in raising our children into adults, we must be willing to give them the opportunities to make mistakes so they can learn from them as well.

This leads us to the point when we need to reflect on our relationship with God. Although many of us act out of love, sometimes we are unwilling to let go and allow our youth to grow up to become adults. Due to the fact that our Korean heritage calls us to support and provide for our children even into adulthood, we tend to treat our youth as children longer than we should. This phenomenon has gotten worse with some parents going with their college students to sign up for classes and some even accompany them to their first job interview! These parents are often called "hover" or "helicopter" parents due to the constant attachment to their child's life. Despite their good intentions, this can greatly influence and hinder social development.

Good intentions are only half the battle. Proper execution is the other half, which the next chapter will cover.

Things to Consider

1. What is your main desire and goal for your child? Do you have biblical support for that goal?
2. Are you raising up your child to be an adult?
3. Do you have control issues? Could this possibly affect the way that you raise up your children?

CHAPTER 5
The Importance of Being a Genuine Christian Parent

"Not everyone who says to me, 'Lord, Lord,' will enter the kingdom of heaven, but only the one who does the will of my Father who is in heaven. Many will say to me on that day, 'Lord, Lord, did we not prophesy in your name and in your name drive out demons and in your name perform many miracles?' Then I will tell them plainly, 'I never knew you. Away from me, you evildoers!'"
- Matthew 7:21-23

Are you a Christian?

No, really, are you a Christian?

This passage in Matthew 7 is probably one of the scariest passages in the Bible. Jesus is teaching us that someday when we face the Lord, there will be many people who will come to him trying to prove their faith. They will come to him with a list of things that they have done for him in his name, truly believing that they are Christians ready to enter the kingdom of heaven, and yet they hear the dreaded words, "I never knew you." The double cry of, "Lord, Lord!" implies that they believed they had a close relationship with him. They *did* have a huge list of things that they were doing for his name.

There's a big reason why this passage scares me: every time I read it, I think about the current Korean American church.

Perhaps you are offended by such a statement and rightly so. I have just challenged your salvation and relationship with the Lord. However, I believe those who are really saved by Christ Jesus will *not* be offended, because they recognize the importance of knowing the current condition of one's relationship with God. They remember the apostle Paul's words in Philippians 2:12 to "work out your salvation with fear and trembling", as they never want to be in the same situation as described in Matthew 7.

I say this knowing that there are many solid Korean Christians out there who genuinely love the Lord and will probably agree with what I have to say.

I fear for the current condition of the Korean American church, because I believe many to this day believe that they are entering heaven through their works and busyness rather than by grace through faith in Jesus Christ.

I commend my people for their commitment to certain practices that other ethnicities have only begun to follow, such as early morning prayer, a passion for missions, and commitment to community meetings. I especially love the grandmas in many of the churches that I have grown up in and served. They're always exhibiting their joy for the Lord, and their loyalty by praying for the church and their leaders.

I share these joys with two major concerns that I and many other gospel-centered pastors have in their hearts. Our commitment in serving the church has slowly transformed our faith into a religion of works, and our faithfulness in upholding a high standard has led to a legalistic church culture. To be clear, I do not say this about all Korean American churches nor am I seeking perfection. There are many churches today which include first-generation Koreans who really do understand the importance of seeking a gospel-centered church, where traditions of man have a much lesser priority than sharing the gospel to all nations. Sadly however, many today continue to cling to a "Korean" method in running a church as opposed to a correct biblical one.

The reason why I point this out at the risk of potentially offending many, is that the souls of many people, including yours, is at stake. The goal of Christianity is not to reach comfort or feeling good about ourselves, but rather obedience to what God has actually said about his church, salvation, and the proper way of living. Let us not make the mistake of Matthew 7:21-23 and assume that everything is ok! For the sake of our souls, our children's souls, and anyone else we love, let's take the time to be honest with ourselves and with the Lord and truly seek genuine Christian faith. This is the first step in working toward restoring your relationship with your family. I pray that the following gospel message is something that you not only know in your mind, but also believe and trust with your heart and reflect through your transformed lifestyle.

There are two passages that I would like to cover to give us insight into the faith that Jesus Christ wants us to follow. The aforementioned Matthew 7:21-23 as well as the entire chapter of Matthew 23.

The seventh chapter of Matthew contains the closing remarks of Jesus' sermon on the mount. If you ever desired a concise sermon that talked about what the Christian life should look like, then I encourage you to read through Matthew 5-7. In chapter 7, verses 21 to 23, Jesus briefly gives us a preview of what the day of judgment will look like. For some reason, even though it seems like there are people who genuinely believed that they had a saving relationship with the Lord, they are condemned, and are not allowed to enter the kingdom of heaven. Depending on your current beliefs, this may sound very strange to you. Some people believe that our entrance to heaven is based on how many good things we do, especially within the church.

Those who truly understand the gospel message of Jesus Christ, know that this is not the case. We are not saved by our works, we are not granted entrance to heaven because of our spiritual resumes, but we are saved by one thing: faith in what Jesus Christ has done for us. There are many verses that support this truth. Ephesians 2:8-9 says clearly, "For by grace you have been saved through faith. And this is not your own doing; it is the gift of God, not a result of works, so that no one may boast." Additionally, Romans 11:6 says, "But if it is by grace, it is no longer on the basis of works; otherwise grace would no longer be grace." Over and over again, we see teachings in the Bible that speaks about how our salvation is not measured by how many good things that we have done, but by faith alone in what Christ has done for us on the cross. In fact, this is one of the things that we see in the Old Testament. The Israelites repeatedly fall into sin, despite the numerous acts of mercy and judgment from God. This points to the truth that the heart of man is wicked and does not want to truly seek God. Man will only desire God when through His mercy, He gives us a new heart in Christ (Ezekiel 36:26). Only then would we begin to have the desires to obey him and love him.

Frankly speaking, I believe a good number of us who attend church do understand and know of this concept that grace alone saves us, but the point of reflection is whether or not we are actually living a lifestyle that shows the gospel truth. Speaking as someone who has interacted with numerous people over the years, I can say one thing for sure: we're really good at distorting the good things from God into something selfish. For example, in Mark 2 and Luke 6, we see a narrative of Jesus and His disciples on the sabbath day, picking up grains from the field to eat. The Pharisees in their legalistic ways, condemned them for "breaking God's commandment" (even though they were not). Jesus offers an example of King David eating holy bread that was only set aside for priests to eat (1 Samuel 21:6). Jesus then makes the remark, "The Sabbath was made for man, not man for the Sabbath."

Jesus is making two important points here. First, the Pharisees were wrong in their creation of extra unnecessary burdens concerning the Sabbath. The Sabbath was originally instituted by God at creation so that man could rest and reflect on his relationship with God. It was not meant to be another day where we were to uphold traditions and worry about fulfilling religious responsibilities. Secondly, the Pharisees had forgotten the intention and purpose of the laws. Upholding the commandments of God was not done out of obligation. They were given to us to show how we could love God and love others (Matthew 22:40). If we obsess over fulfilling the commandments while forgetting to love one another and those in need, we are missing the purpose of the law (1 Corinthians 13).

Have we as Koreans, in our high standards and expectations, slowly transformed the purpose of church, our faith and our understanding of Christianity in this manner? Are our churches places of grace and restoration, or places where we are constantly scrutinizing others to uphold a certain reputation? To be clear, standards are not bad (Matthew 23:2-3) but we must reflect on whether we are forgetting the main intent of the law. I say this knowing that no church is perfect, but let's not let that be an excuse for our behavior. When we consider that a lot of us who have migrated to America came to the church with intentions of networking first and worshipping second, is it possible that over time, we have forgotten the real purpose of the church?

We can test and reflect on this matter ourselves. When there was a scandal in the church, did we personally make the effort to confront and restore them from their sin as it says in Galatians 6:1 and Matthew 18? Does it feel like we fall back onto our Korean habits and avoid getting involved because it is "none of our business"? How do we respond to the smaller things such as the way we dress, the cars that we drive, which school so-and-so's children got into and so forth? Do these things seem to take higher priority and concern more than the condition of your relationship with the Lord? Ultimately, it comes down to the question of whether or not we measure the condition of our faith by the things that we do and have. If that is the case, we might be in trouble.

As I study scripture, it's quite amazing to see the similarities that Koreans have with the Israelites in the Old Testament. We have gone through hardships, sometimes being displaced from our motherland, and yet there are those who remain faithful despite the difficulties that we go through. Sadly however, we also carry similar issues that the Israelites had with their walks with God.

For example, one deception that a lot of Jews believed in back in the day was when one was blessed with material blessing and wealth, the Lord was happy with them and therefore gave them all of these things. As long as our physical lives were good, then there was nothing to worry about. However, this was *exactly* the problem that the Old Testament prophets warned about. In their beliefs and the comfort of their wealth, they had forgotten to take care of the poor and the widows, and had turned a blind eye to injustices going on in their cities. The Lord warned them to turn around before they were judged, yet many times, Israel went off to worship other gods, never admitting that they were wrong, forgetting about the true God.

Have we too, as the Korean church, focused so much about on the conditions of life that we have ended up ignoring our true calling as Christians? Have we idolized money and success at the cost of our relationship with God to the extent that we are committing the same sins as the Jews did back in the day?

In Matthew 23, Jesus strongly condemns the Pharisees for their hypocrisy and the negative influence that they have had over the people they were to lead. Let the Word of God speak to you as you consider these teaching points alongside where you stand in your Christian faith.

> v. 2-4– "The scribes and the Pharisees sit on Moses' seat, so do and observe whatever they tell you, but not the works they do. For they preach, but do not practice. They tie up heavy burdens, hard to bear, and lay them

on people's shoulders, but they themselves are not willing to move them with their finger.

v. 5 – They do all their deeds to be seen by others. For they make their phylacteries broad and their fringes long, and they love the place of honor at feasts and the best seats in the synagogues and greetings in the marketplaces and being called rabbi by others.

v. 23 – Woe to you scribes and Pharisees, hypocrites! For you tithe mint and dill and cumin and have neglected the weightier matters of the law: justice and mercy and faithfulness. These you ought to have done, without neglecting the others.

v. 24 – You blind guides, straining out a gnat and swallowing a camel!

v. 25 – Woe to you, scribes and Pharisees, hypocrites! For you clean the outside of the cup and the plate, but inside they are full of greed and self-indulgence.

v. 27-28 – Woe to you, scribes and Pharisees, hypocrites! For you are like whitewashed tombs, which outwardly appear beautiful, but within are full of dead people's bones and all uncleanness. So you also outwardly appear righteous to others, but within you are full of hypocrisy and lawlessness."

As we can see, our Lord was very serious about having the proper relationship with God. The main issue that Jesus had with these Pharisees was that even though they were doing the motions of worship, the intentions and the hearts behind them were selfish in nature. How often do I think about verse 5 sometimes as I serve in Korean churches today! Some churches even list in the church bulletin the names of people who gave their tithes and offering in the previous weeks. They boast about how much they have done inside the walls of the church, yet do nothing to help those who are truly in need (v. 23). Many still focus heavily on outside appearances, the latest accomplishments of their child, or the conditions of their businesses, while having little to no concern over the hearts of the people.

Let's consider the Corinthian church. Corinth was a well-known city of trade with many overlapping cultures and beliefs. Due to this melting pot of worldviews, many ungodly beliefs and practices seeped into the church. There was a man who was sleeping with his stepmother (1 Corinthians 5), people were treating the Lord's supper as a time to eat, drink and party (ch. 11), and many were abusing spiritual gifts to draw attention to themselves rather than edifying the church (chs.12-14). What we see in the church of Corinth are people who base the practices of the church on their cultural habits rather than on God's Word. Thank goodness that the Lord used the apostle Paul to write letters demanding an end to these practices!

I share these things not out of bitterness, but out of broken-heartedness. I plea for those who read through these passages to honestly reflect over the issues within their own church. I think I can confidently say that most of us have at one point said, "That's just simply how Korean churches are sometimes." Please, let us not just pessimistically accept the idea that we are so bound by our culture and traditions that we cannot change. No, I believe that in Christ, we can do all things that work toward his glory and his kingdom (Philippians 4:13), and even the hardest of hearts can change to genuinely follow our Lord.

I pray that we no longer hold firm to a false Christianity that is based on works, but rather embrace the true gospel that is grounded in grace. Let us seek a biblical Christian faith that seeks to love people made in the image of God, rather than loving them for their titles, positions, and accomplishments. There are many other detailed concerns we could go over, but they point back to the main idea: Are we measuring our faith by our works, or by what Jesus Christ wants in our life, our hearts and devotion to Him? Let us no longer live a "Christian faith" where we try to prove our faith to ourselves, to God and to others in the church by earning favor within the church. Let us *love* Christ first so that all acts of worship and service are *byproducts* of our love.

Genuine Christianity means worshipping God in spirit and in truth (John 4:24). "Spirit", implying that there is an actual transformation in the heart by the Spirit of God that causes us to be born again (John 3:3-8) and make us into new creation (2 Corinthians 5:17). "Truth", implying that we worship according to God's standards not ours. True faith is one that follows and loves his commandments (John 14:15, 21, 23; 1 John 2:3). Christ is showing us that a genuine love for him *leads* to acts of love and worship. When we worship out of love not of obligation, then Christianity as a whole becomes a joy, rather than a burden. Our love for Christ makes it easy for us to follow and obey him as opposed to one that works hard in trying to earn favor of God through our works (Matthew 11:28-30).

I hope we are beginning to see the dangers of following "cultural Christianity" as opposed to a biblical Christianity. One is done out of obligation and one is done out of adoration. One seeks to earn favor and salvation from God, while the other receives it freely because Christ has already paid the price! False Christianity enslaves us back into a system of works and rituals, while true Christianity gives us freedom because Christ has forgiven all of our sins and given us his righteousness. I pray that we fall into the latter category and have truly given our lives to the true gospel. Even though we were sinners, Christ who was without sin died for us. (Romans 5:8; 2 Corinthians 5:21) The more we recognize how much the Lord loves us truly, we too will begin to live a life of grace, genuine love, and service in truth.

If we truly want a genuine relationship with our children, where we can understand their ways, love them, and raise them up properly and in a godly manner, we must first accept the real gospel of Jesus Christ. If this chapter was music to your ears and you understand what I have said, then praise God, you're on the right track! If not however, I pray that this becomes a reality for you as you continue to read through this book. Do whatever you can to find the answers to the questions you have today, whether through your pastors or by other gospel-centered teachers.

Because now we will be diving into even more difficult and potentially offensive things.

Things to Consider
1. What are your thoughts on the passage of Matthew 7:21-23?
2. Why is it important that we are assured in our own faith before considering the faith of others, including our children?
3. How does our love for Christ help us love others?

CHAPTER 6
The Cost of Christian Parenting

> *"If anyone comes to me and does not hate his own father and mother and wife and children and brothers and sisters, yes, and even his own life, he cannot be my disciple."*
> *– Luke 14:26*

Here's a little experiment: show that verse above to Korean people and record their responses.

In the context of that verse, Jesus is teaching his hearers about the cost of discipleship; what it actually entails to be called a genuine Christian. He certainly starts off with a hard-hitter doesn't he? Let's be careful not to misunderstand what Jesus is saying here; let's study the context. As mentioned, Jesus is discussing the realities of being an actual Christian. He is sharing the fact that it is difficult, not easy, and costly, not comfortable. Verse 27 says, "Whoever does not carry his own cross cannot be my disciple." Furthermore, he takes the time to share examples of people who "counted the cost" before coming to a decision (v. 28-32). The same reality applies to the Christian life today. To become a genuine follower of Christ should not necessarily be a simple decision. It is one that potentially costs your entire life, figuratively and literally. When we read verse 26 in the context of what Jesus is teaching, we can understand that the cost of being a Christian can even include sacrificing the relationships with our close family members.

This can be extremely offensive to the traditional conservative Korean who grew up in a Confucius background, especially if they are one who has been brought up believing that even within Christianity, we are taught to honor and obey our parents. The main point that Christ is teaching us, as shown throughout scripture, is that your relationship with the Lord is the most important thing in your life. It is more important than the government, your political leaning, your hobbies and jobs, money and your earthly desires, and yes, even more than your relationships. Simply put, none of those things listed above can save us eternally nor fully satisfy us in life. This is the blessing behind a truth that is hard to swallow. The more we accept this truth that Christ is the most important thing in life and we begin to trust in His ways, we actually end up with more blessed relationships, a better understanding of money, a better response to the circumstances in life, and a better view of how life works in general. This is probably one of the key points that we as Koreans must accept if we are to ever jump to the point of strong, genuine, and authentic Christianity. This is the foundation that we must begin our faith with, as Christ taught us to build our house upon the rock (his Word) rather than the sand (our plans) (Matthew 7:24-27).

Let's take a step outside of the Korean world for some further insight. I've been blessed to partner alongside many missionaries around the world. It's always difficult to hold in my tears whenever I hear some of their testimonies of coming to Christ. One group in particular are my brothers and sisters who were former Muslims but came to the Lord through extraordinary circumstances. In many countries in the middle east, even though it may not be advertised as such, the penalty for being a Christian is death. Many are beaten, raped, and even killed when their family members or neighbors find out that they have converted from Islam to Christianity. I have seen pictures and spoken to many brothers who have the literal scars on their bodies and stories of the torture that they have gone through. The descriptions of the jail cells that they have been in can make anyone shudder. Despite the cost, the literal cost of running away from their families, their homes, and even their physical safety, they have given their lives to the Lord. These dramatic stories may seem surreal, but they are genuine, and they act as a living example of Luke 14:26. It's not that these newborn Christians hate their mothers or fathers, but their love for Jesus Christ is so great, they are willing to give up their family connection to follow him.

Many of our Korean youth live with a similar fear, but in a Korean context, the reality of honor and shame. Many of our youth today who want to follow Christ are constantly torn between the desire of following Christ and the cost of bringing "shame and dishonor" to their parents. Again, how would you personally respond if and when your child expressed a desire to enter ministry? Would you believe there are many today who want to truly give their lives to Christ and his kingdom but are held back by the fear of upsetting their parents?

Perhaps one reoccurring tragedy that I've seen many times in my life is when a child gives his or her life to the Lord and wants to be baptized, but to their dismay, instead of a joyful response, their parents are offended or upset. The parents claim that they were already Christian "since birth", and argue that there is no real reason to get baptized. Some parents even demand that their child be more passionate about school than Christianity.

How would we personally respond in these scenarios? Based on what we have discussed on the concept of genuine Christianity and a "cultural Christianity", what do you believe the Lord expects out of us? The purpose of these points is to present the idea that as there is a cost in living a genuine Christian life. These things also encompass the way that we raise our children.

The Lord says it clearly when he creates the first couple here on this earth, "a man shall leave his father and mother, and hold fast to his wife, and they shall become one flesh" (Genesis 2:24). Part of discipling our children is understanding that one day, they will become an adult. For them to grow into a biblical man or woman, they too must leave the protection and care of their parents to start their own family, and to be a loving and supporting spouse, or an independent single adult. I understand that this promotion of independence seems very western by nature and perhaps even anti-Korean at face value. Realistically speaking, although we will always be the mother or father of our child, we will not be their caretaker forever. Let's also consider the fact that they must survive in a western culture with expectations which are different from ours. I briefly mentioned the concept of a "hover parent", there *are* negative repercussions of an attached parenting style where we believe that through our efforts and work, we will determine the fate of our children. I'm not denying that the way we raise up our youth definitely impacts their maturity later on, but we have to discern how realistic this actually is.

When we stop and reflect on how many things there are in life that are outside of our control, we can respond in two ways: in utter paralyzing fear which leads to sheltering our kids forever, or trust in a sovereign God who *does* have everything under control. In fact, an attached parenting style is actually a sign of a lack of faith and trust in the Lord. The reality is, we *will not* be around forever and we don't even know the number of our days. This is not an excuse to refrain from giving it our all for our children, but a reminder to remember our limitedness and to trust the Lord. As difficult as it is to not reach out and ease the pain that your children experience we must allow them to go through hardships so that they may grow in endurance (Romans 5:3; James 1:3), build godliness (2 Peter 1:7), build a genuine faith (1 Peter 4:12-19), and most importantly, have a trusting relationship with the Lord! Do we believe that it is Jesus alone who saves? Then we need to raise our children to trust in Him more than in us. Let's work toward a parenting style that always reveals to our children our need for Christ!

Every single one of us has a unique life and calling given to us but what we believe to be the best for our children may not be what the Lord says. Will we continue to trust in assumptions, generalizations, and cultural traditions in raising up our children, or will we allow them to live a story that only the Lord can write for them? Will we speak out truth, yet live in hypocrisy, or will we seek to be like Christ, not only speaking truth, but also living the gospel in our lives?

God loves the world and whoever believes in his Son will not perish but will have eternal life (John 3:16). We also should remember that our God is a personal God who gives us his personal time and has a unique calling for all of us in his plans. (Hebrews 13:20-21; Psalm 119:105; James 1:5; Psalm 139:14; Matthew 10:30, etc.) If our Heavenly Father treats us so uniquely, then should we not also give unique care to our children, as unique individuals? Let us not treat them as mere robots where we search for the "correct" general cure-all that has them perform the behavior that best satisfies us.

We are called to care for our children in the ways of the Lord (Proverbs 22:6)[14]; we're called to train them in godly truth and not provoke them to anger or frustration (Ephesians 6:4). The best way to do this is not by domineering over them, demanding nothing but expectations without any discussion, but by being a model for the behavior that you expect out of them. I like how one of my friends in ministry puts it: teenagers have a very good radar for hypocrisy. They can quickly detect if you're being real or not. The way they do this is by simply measuring your words with your actions. Part of this is due to the western culture, where individuals judge others regardless of their age. Many westerners do not have the Confucius buffer that protects them from the

---

14 There are people who interpret this in a slightly different manner (but the same truth!). They believe this verse is saying that however you raise your child in their youth, that's the behavior that they will stick to as they become an adult.

scrutiny of the younger generation. All in all, don't we enjoy time with a person of integrity rather than a person who lacks commitment?

Wouldn't our children expect the same?

Paul teaches Titus to lead men into teaching younger men not by just their words, but through their lives. "Exercise self-control, to be worthy of respect and to live wisely. They must have sound faith and be filled with love and patience" (Titus 2:2). Women are equally expected to "live in a way that honors God." Notice that the first step in teaching the younger generation is to make sure that we have things correct first! Jesus taught us that before we judge the speck in our brother's eye, we need to check out the large stick or plank in our own eye. It is impossible for the blind to lead the blind (Luke 6:39). Furthermore, our Lord warned spiritual leaders against seemingly being righteous on the outside, but spiritually dead and hypocritical on the inside (Matthew 23:27-28).

We see throughout scripture that there is a need to model godly behavior, not just simply demand things with our words. That's quite a contrast from the unquestioned family loyalty that Confucius expected out of us! We should also consider other factors such as the reality that our youth grow up in a western culture that focuses on independence and finding an identity that distinguishes one's self from the family group. They tend to find identities through their interactions with their peers, their accomplishments, and their calling.

To focus on the main point, ask again, where do our standards of raising our children come from? Why do we trust in our current method to be true? Lastly, and probably the most important question pertaining to our subject, is it possible that our plans (with good intentions) simply do not apply as well to our children today due to the differences in culture and expectations? Is it possible that the mere fear of losing our Korean heritage, a secondary attribute of who we are, causes us to desperately cling onto outdated beliefs and methods that do not understand contemporary culture?

Let's love our children as *our* children, gifted to us from our Lord.

Points of Reflection
Work Toward a Healthy Marriage

One of the most overlooked factors in raising up healthy children today is found within our own marriages. Although we may be eager to work towards raising up our children in the ways of the Lord, if we do not have a healthy relationship with our spouses, we are already at a huge disadvantage. Consider some of the effects divorce has over children:

- Higher dropout rate from school
- Higher rate of teen pregnancy
- Three times more likely to have emotional and behavioral problems.
- 20-30% more likely to have health issues[15]

When we offer two voices that speak truth and guidance to our children, the effects can be profound. There are certain cares that a mother can give to their child that a father cannot and vice versa. When we work toward a parenting partnership, we are following the model and structure that our Lord intended when it comes to the family. I encourage you to partner with your spouse as much as possible in raising your child. Your youth are *both* of your responsibility![16]

Children First Belong to the Lord

Remember that question that I asked you to reflect on concerning how you would respond if your child desired to enter ministry? It's time to answer that question. I've had my fair share of parents who have asked me to speak and "counsel" their child *not* to enter ministry. It's ironic, because they are praying and asking God for things that

---

15 Stanton, Glenn T. Why Marriage Matters: Reasons to Believe in Marriage in Post-Modern Society. Colorado Springs, CO: Pinon Press.

16 I acknowledge that some of my readers have already divorced or are currently in a difficult relationship with their spouse. I urgently encourage you not to keep marital problems to yourselves but to seek help! This is exactly where the church can come in to offer support and encouragement. If your church does not offer this type of encouragement, then seek another church you can trust that would offer counseling. There is no shame in receiving help in this area. For your wellbeing as well as that of your children, do what you can to receive help from others!

go against God. Understandably, many Asian parents do not want their child to go through suffering and hardship which typically come within the ministry and they desire a more "comfortable" life for their kin, because they themselves have usually gone through major hardships growing up as well. There is nothing wrong with seeking peace and comfort for future generations. What good parent would casually and nonchalantly send their child into areas of risk? However, there are two questions we need to be asking ourselves.

Firstly, can any amount of anxiety, fear, preparation and protection set in stone the paths for our children to walk upon?

"Many are the plans in the mind of a man, but it is the purpose of the Lord that will stand" (Proverbs 19:21).

"The lot is cast into the lap, but its every decision is from the LORD" (Proverbs 16:33).

Our Lord also tells us not to worry about tomorrow (Matthew 6:25-34). These are fairly well-known verse among churches today, and present the loving care of our heavenly Father over us. We are worth much more than the birds in the sky (v. 26) and the lilies of the field (v. 28). There is no amount of anxiety that can actually change or impact what will happen to us in the future. (v. 27) Jesus encourages us to just focus on one thing: Being faithful to what is given to us today for that is already enough work (v. 34).

Additionally, in Luke 12:12-31, Jesus speaks on the parable of the "rich fool," where a man had the problem of "having too much." The man chooses to break down all of his small barns to build himself a huge barn, in order to store all of his harvest. After spending a considerable amount of time investing in his future and finally completing his goals, he dies. Quite a tragedy in one sense, but a constant possibility in our everyday lives.

The author of Ecclesiastes can also relate. He says in 2:18-19,

"I hated all my toil in which I toil under the sun, seeing that I must leave it to the man who will come after me,

and who knows whether he will be wise or a fool? Yet he will be master of all for which I toiled and used my wisdom under the sun. This also is vanity."

Here was this man who had the rare chance of actually having everything one could want: money, power, and even pleasure. He also had the privilege of being able to live out different paths to discover the purpose of life and each one ended up in utter disappointment. He discovered that even a life of hard work and diligence was worthless, because you never knew when it would all come to an end, preventing you from actually enjoying the fruits of your labors.

To quote the famous Christian apologist Ravi Zacharias, "The loneliest moment in life is when you have just experienced that which you thought would deliver the ultimate and it has just let you down."

Does this not unfortunately describe many of the lifestyles of the Korean community today? Is it possible that through our capacity to endure suffering with hard work, for the sake of providing a better world for our youth, that we have forgotten more important matters in life? Is it possible that because of our focus on the goal that we have created for ourselves, we have miscalculated hidden factors which impact the way we raise up our children?

The main point we must consider is this: no matter what the good intentions may be, no matter how much we are willing to endure, and no matter how much we can plan and prepare, it is the Lord and his will that will come to pass. This applies to how we raise up our children as well.

We can spend hours agonizing late into the night, frantically worrying if our children will come home. We can presumptuously attempt to shelter our children from all dangers and temptations in the world. We can continue to domineer our children regarding academics, treating them as numbers rather than unique individual. The further we continue to do these things, this will be the outcome: creating a vessel or even an idol so that others take notice, and thus give us the glory. Will we continue to sacrifice the spiritual and emotional wellbeing of our children as a source for our own boasting? How much longer will we disguise our selfish desires with "good intentions concerning their future wellbeing?"

We must recognize that we too are limited beings whom are imperfect, sinful, and sometimes blind to our own flaws. We must instead trust in the Lord and his ways, even if they make us uncomfortable, especially in the way that we raise our children. They belong to him first, not to us!

Secondly, we must reflect on whether or not we are hindering the work of God in our children. Has our good-intentioned focus on academics and financial success upon our children ended up interfering with their spiritual growth? Consider the well-known parable of the sower in Matthew 13. Jesus speaks of how a sower went out to the field to plant some seeds. Some of the seeds fell on the sidewalk and were eaten by birds, others fell on rocky soil, some fell in the thorns and then finally good soil. For those who are unaware of the meaning of this parable, Christ is teaching us that the Word of God is the seed while our hearts are the different types of soil. Some who hear God's word will reject it immediately, while others will hear it, be quickly excited for it but then run away at the first hint of hardship. The one that I feel particularly applies to many of our Korean communities is the thorns. Jesus explains to us in verse 22, that the thick, thorny branches represent the worries of the world and the "deceitfulness of riches." People are so concerned over their financial wellbeing and success that they are distracted and cannot fully commit to the Lord.

Jesus touches upon this subject in another passage where he meets with a foolish rich man. This man claimed that he upheld all the commandments and was worthy to enter the kingdom of heaven. However, Jesus offers him one challenge, to go sell all of his possessions, give the money to the poor and then come follow him. The rich man is unable to do so and leaves in sorrow. Jesus summarizes this event with his famous imagery, "It is easier for a camel to enter through the eye of the needle than a rich person to enter the kingdom of God" (Matthew

19:24). Christ isn't teaching us that it is impossible for rich people to enter heaven, but that those who live a life of luxury, also live a life of anxiety, because they have so many concerns over their things.[17]

These two points along with what we have covered so far further strengthen the theme that we as the first and first-and-a-half Korean generation must be willing to accept the fact that the transition of our geographical location must also introduce a transition in our cultural expectations. Our children must not only face the normal challenges of growing into adolescence and eventual adulthood, but must also grow within a context where two separate cultures are fighting with each other in contributing to their identity. Hopefully, an understanding and acceptance of these realities can help us see the blessings of entrusting our children to the Lord. It can feel very foreign to us especially with our tendency as Koreans to affirm ownership over things because we have worked so hard for them, but biblically everything actually belongs to the Lord and that includes our children (Hebrews 2:10; Psalm 127:3). The good news is, our Lord takes care of his children very seriously. Mark 9:37 and 10:14 show us what God thinks about children, even encouraging believers to have the faith of a "child" to enter the kingdom of heaven. Additionally, in Matthew 18, he makes it very clear that we are to care for them and if anybody causes them to sin, the punishment that follows will be very severe. If children are given to us as a gift from God, (Psalm 127:3) how will we treat the gift that has been entrusted to us? May we be a positive and godly influence over them!

Our Children Need Relationships More Than Nice Things

In Ephesians 6:1, children are given a command to honor their parents. This commandment comes with a promise because generally, children who do take the advice and wisdom from their elders will live a better, safer and healthier life. It's simple, but it makes a lot of

---

17 "Better is a little with the fear of the LORD than great treasure and trouble with it." – Proverbs 15:16

sense – when you listen to those who have experience, you can learn from their successes and mistakes!

Sadly, we have taken that verse out of context and simply use it to demand respect and submission from our children. However, if we read the next verse it says, "Fathers, do not exasperate your children" or simply put, do not anger your children. Instead, raise them up in the training and instruction of the Lord.

Verse 2 illuminates verse 1, especially the concern of honoring and obeying parents coming with a promise. If children are expected to obey their parents for it does lead to a safer, wiser life, then parents have the responsibility to provide that teaching and nurture for them.

This brings up the question: What is the best way to carry this out? If we genuinely want to offer the best for them not just in tangible things, but in spiritual matters, there is one answer.

In my 10 plus years of working with youth in a ministry context, 5 years in a teaching context, counseling numerous people over this period of time, studying numerous books and articles on the subject, listening to years of conference speakers about youth ministries and the like, it all comes down to one word:

RELATIONSHIP

Throughout scripture, we are called to become followers of Christ, or in other words, disciples of Christ. A disciple is one who lives a life following the doctrines of another. In the famous passage known as the "Great Commission", Jesus teaches us that the main calling of all Christians is to go into the world, making disciples and *teaching* them to observe and obey everything that he has taught us (Matthew 28:18-20). Fortunately for us, there is no greater teacher than Jesus our Lord. If we follow his methods, we should not be surprised when we find more and more people connecting with us on a deeper level, especially our own children.

One of the outstanding themes that exist within discipleship is the intentional investment of spending time with others and building up relationships with them. The depth of any relationship, whether a friendship, business partnership, or even a marriage, is greatly determined by the willingness each side has in investing in the other.

Consider people in your life who have left an impact on you in some positive way. Perhaps it was a school teacher who believed in you and put great efforts into helping you academically. If we have ever wondered where our children get some of their 'strange' views and habits from, let's reflect on the fact that many of our children spend a majority of their adolescent years *away from us* due to academics and extracurricular activities. Let's not deny the reality that certain teachers do not simply teach academics but can also instill their beliefs and ideals which clash with our Korean heritage. Do not forget about the peers your children spend time with in and out of school, who will also share their personal views on matters of life. Constantly throughout the day, our youth are bombarded with various views which may or may not match with ours nor with the Bible.

Similarly, there might have been a relative who took care of you as you were growing up because your parents were busy at work to provide for the family. Perhaps there was that good friend who was always with you when things became difficult. There is a good chance that the reason why these people are close to you is because they have invested time and effort in serving and loving you and pointing you to a better direction in life. In our current culture that demands that our youth find themselves, our youth will lean toward those who they trust and feel comfortable with. In general, those who spend the most time with them and show authenticity with their words as well as their actions, have the greatest impact on them.

If we expect our youth to grow up with certain standards, we must be the ones who invest time in close proximity to build up a trusting relationship so that they are willing to receive our input. We hold the responsibility in raising them to be mature worshippers of God. This requires discipleship and a trusting relationship that comes with time and the willingness to entrust them to the Lord's calling when the time comes.

For some of us this is very difficult, specifically those who have grown up without a loving father figure, but a lack of personal experience is no excuse for us to fail to equip ourselves in breaking a cycle which exists among many Korean families here in America. It seems daunting, especially when we see the amount of culture that we must assimilate to even begin to understand our children. But let me encourage you, it is possible! Not only do we have the Lord with us, but when I reflect on the amount of resources that we have to help us in this calling as parents, we are without excuse. To be frank, the failure to adapt to understand the adolescent culture in America is not due to the lack of resources, but rather an unwillingness to trust and attempt to understand.

Our youth need someone who can encourage, guide, and offer structure in their life. Sure, it may feel like the current path that they walk on seems to only satisfy themselves. However, just as we have gone through growing pains, they too will eventually ponder the bigger things in life, such as their purpose, significant relationships, and identity.

It's a reflection of what the author of Ecclesiastes ponders in his entire book. What *is* the purpose of life? He had the opportunity to have it all – money, power, and relationships and yet he realized that it was all meaningless. As our children slowly reach the age of maturity and realize that their childish ways were a waste of time, they *will* be seeking answers to the questions that come to their hearts. The fact of the matter is, they will listen to those whom they feel closest to and those with whom they can entrust their deepest secrets and struggles. Our youth are willing to trust in those they believe have the best intentions for them. Those type of relationships can only exist when someone has put in the effort to walk life beside them, showing them love and support, and proving to them through their words as well as their actions that they want the best for them. Hopefully we're beginning to understand the inefficiency of simply lecturing our children.

Remember our friend Christopher Langan? I believe that due to the lack of solid mentors in his upbringing, he allowed his life to drift in to mediocrity. He had the skills, the capability, but no drive. Drive usually comes from an intentional investment from a mentor figure. Let us break free from our cultural tendency of believing that giving our children a strong academic background alone is sufficient in their upbringing.

Fortunately for us, discussing these issues offers us good insight into what type of relationship we should be offering to our children. The concept of "having a relationship" with your child varies from person to person. Unfortunately, some people seek to become very lenient and strive to be that "cool parent" who allows their children to have parties, freedom, and will even drink together. This is not our intention. What we encourage and remind parents again to consider is to understand that you have a unique relationship with your child and although there are certain general guidelines that we can follow in raising them up, you will have a unique story with your child as their parent. Due to these reasons, as well as the complexities that come within parenting, this is the best "generalized" answer that I can offer. **Our youth need structured and genuine relationships.**

By structured, I mean an environment that sets clear guidelines, boundaries, and expectations with consistency. God's Word accomplishes this perfectly. Scripture sufficiently teaches everything that we need to know about life including our origin, purpose, our relationship with others, and our eternal destination (2 Timothy 3:16). The church as well as youth pastors (which we'll touch upon later!) are there to help supplement and keep us accountable in carrying out our calling as biblical parents. Other Christian parents are also our source of encouragement and are shoulders to lean on when parenting becomes difficult.

By genuine, I mean that we are not called to put on a show or "parent face", but to walk beside our kids in honesty and openness, confessing our mistakes and failures and striving to do right the next time. This concept may be foreign to us as Asians who have inherited an expectation of respect and submission from our children. However, the goal here is not to encourage our kids to give up their Korean identity, but to show them that our Korean heritage comes secondary to our identities in Christ. It is a realization that even our good intentions as well as our culture is insufficient when it comes to explaining every aspect of life and trusting in our Creator who is perfectly capable of doing so. When we admit our mistakes to our children, we are showing them the greatest priority is to make things right with God, not to be the "best Korean". Spending time with them in conversation, even when it may seem foolish shows that you are investing in them as Christ did with his followers. When we involve them in our worship, showing them our love for Christ in both the home *and* with the church, we are showing them that Christianity is not an obligation, but a genuine saving relationship with God.

This is not a promise, as there are always exceptions, but in the same spirit of Proverbs 22:6, let us seek to train up and raise our children in the ways of the Lord by investing in a *relationship* with our child, so that when they get older they will not depart from it. This is the key.

Hebrews 4:15 shows us that Jesus Christ is the best priest because he is able to empathize with us in every way. If we are to model Christ, the best teacher, then we should be looking for a parenting style that's more than just "knowing the Bible" or "knowing the answer." The same applies to pastors who are expected to not only know the word but "do" the word (James 1:22). Seek those who genuinely want the best for the spiritual upbringing of our youth. If we seek pastors who simply babysit or entertain our youth at church, then do not be surprised when these youth leave for other things. When it comes to offering entertainment and pleasure, the world will always beat the church every single time. Let's offer something much more different and life-giving, the gospel truth of Jesus Christ that brings answers, purpose, and life.

Christians are called to be countercultural, even in the way we bring up our children. Let's disciple them to be a source of truth and hope rather than another number in society. We have seen numerous tragedies and misconducts of adults throughout time and society and I will boldly say that a majority of them stem from the way that person was raised in childhood. Studies show that children from divorced families have a higher chance of getting divorced. In regard to influence, the same is true for alcoholism, drugs, gambling, and other habits. The third commandment gives us very good insight, the sins of the fathers *do* pass down to future generations (Exodus 20:5). Let us not make the mistake of trading the truth for current misconceptions which "feel good" but in actuality have long term repercussions that we won't be able to see until many years later. What we sow today, we *will* reap later! (Galatians 6:7)

It is my prayer that Korean American parents will begin their journey in raising their child by looking at their *own* relationship with Christ first. We can only offer the best for our child when we first experience what's best.

Things to Consider

1. How does the reality of our children belonging first to the Lord impact the way that you look at them?
2. Do you raise up your child in a way that reflects control over their lives or submission to God's authority?
3. Who are other parents that you know and trust to raise their children in the ways of the Lord? How is your current relationship with them?

To First-Generation Korean Pastors

CHAPTER 7
What is Your Vision for Your Church?

"A fool takes no pleasure in understanding, but only in expressing his opinion."
 - Proverbs 18:2

In 1876, Western Union was the leader of the communications industry. After observing the newly invented "telephone" they came to the conclusion that it had too many shortcomings and thus had no value in the business.

In 1932, Albert Einstein, the well-known physicist said, "There is not the slightest indication that nuclear energy will ever be obtainable."

Back in 1981, Bill Gates, billionaire founder of Microsoft, stated that computers would never need more than 640 kilobytes of memory. Today, the common entry-level computer holds three to six gigabytes, which is roughly 6×10^6 more powerful.[18]

We may chuckle at these statements today, but only with the benefit of retrospect. All of these views, however, were considered the norm at the time. Many of today's societal views are just as likely

---
18 These facts are paraphrased from the book, *Uncommon Character: Stories of Ordinary Men and Women Who have Done the Extraordinary.* Douglas Feavel, p. *150*

to change. Just think about the number of news reports covering the ever-changing benefits and risks of certain foods, climate change, social movements, and moral views.

There is a term for this tendency to hold firm to certain beliefs simply based on previous experience: apriorism. This is our introduction to the purpose of this chapter.

To be honest, I found it difficult to begin this section of the book. On one hand, the way that I was brought up wants to respect the elders as much as possible, but then on the other hand, I'm convicted to speak the Word of God so clearly, especially to leaders that have been called by the Lord to lead his church. I think the conflict within my heart is a reflection of the struggles that many second and third-generation Korean Americans feel in their churches today. As many of the prophets and apostles in scripture spoke unpopular opinions, I too will offer a respectable but firm argument on the need for discussion concerning many Korean American churches today.

Koreans are in a unique situation. We are sometimes called the "model-minority" due to our academic and socio-economic success despite the hardships that we may have endured. This should come to no surprise as Asians are some of the hardest working ethnic groups to this day. The fact that certain stereotypes exist today such as, "Asians are born doing math in their mother's womb" further cements this view.

However, perhaps due to stereotypes, alongside with pride, stubbornness, misunderstanding of the changing culture, and an unwillingness to adapt, we may have allowed certain unbiblical beliefs and practices to continue. As with many immigrants, we entrap ourselves in a time-bubble within our transition, which simply means we bring over the habits and traditions of the decade we moved away from. If you moved from Korea to the States in the 80's, then your habits, beliefs, and even your worship styles will be very 80's, even if the culture changes in the motherland! It is a prime example of apriorism within the Korean culture today. We are comfortable in the ways that we were taught, even if it means enduring suffering here and there.

Although the number of studies done on the effects immigrating to a new country has on families is fairly young (no more than 30 years), the message is very clear. There are issues within the Korean American community that we can no longer ignore. Furthermore, there is a desperate need in overhauling the visions and methods required in serving the upcoming generations. When studies have shown that there are ongoing issues of drug-use, gang-related activity, intergenerational conflict, and depression[19], it's worth questioning whether or not our current methods in serving our Korean families are still effective and biblical for today.

So with that said, before I get into the bulk of this chapter, this is my one request for any first-generation pastor reading this book: All we ask as the younger generation is *discussion and corporate prayer*. We are not claiming that we are correct all the time, we are not seeking to disrespect our elders or even dismissing our beautiful culture and traditions. What we do ask for is our voice and thoughts to be heard and that we may partner with our elders in serving our Lord.

The biggest frustration that we have as the younger generation is that we feel that our thoughts are immediately shut down and the discouragement this brings eventually leads many of us to burn out and leave the ministry. The purpose of this discussion is that we as the next generation of pastors and Christians would deepen our love for the Lord, and would hold a strong everlasting faith for our future. The goal of this book is not to point out the rights and wrongs, but to raise awareness of issues at hand, challenging both sides to simply compare their current beliefs with scripture, seeking obedience to the Lord first above all things (Matthew 6:10, 33). I strongly believe that the Word of God is timeless, as it explains the heart of man so clearly and is still living and

---

19 1994, Lee, Jee-Sook, "Intergenerational Conflict, Ethnic Identity and Their Influences on Problem Behaviors Among Korean American Adolescents." – University of Pittsburgh School of Social Work.

active today despite the everchanging contexts. Will you, a shepherd called by the Lord, humble yourself before *Him* and the Word of God?

A Reflection on the History of the Korean American Church and Its' Growing Problems Today

Back in 1996, there was a timely article by Helen Lee titled, "The Silent Exodus." It was an article that described the phenomenon happening within Korean churches at that time: the silent departure of youth and young adults from their churches. There were many potential reasons for their departure, but many of those reasons could be summarized as a lack of love from the first generation. Some of the young people felt they were in an overly rigid and legalistic environment that turned them away from the faith. Many kids attended church up to their high school years, but the minute they had freedom in college, they would leave their home church for another or simply leave the church period.

Sadly, although there has been much progress due to the efforts of second and third-generation Korean pastors, many of these issues continue. First-generation leaders must ask themselves if they are aware of this ongoing problem that goes on quietly in the hearts of the younger generations. To make matters worse, many who do have the courage to speak up concerning these issues get shut down, and are often called out as disrespectful and too young to offer any valid opinion.

Earlier in this book, we talked about the influence of Buddhist and Confucius teachings which have seeped into the Korean churches. Although one could pull out the positives from each worldview, we desire that scripture be the ultimate say in the way that we live and worship today.

Let's touch upon an issue of major concern within Korean American churches today – the departure of the youth. Consider some of the attempted solutions that I have observed from first-generation leadership:

- ✦ Create a bigger church building, add a gym or a basketball court; entice students with programs.

- Pile all responsibilities onto the youth/young adult pastor, making him the scapegoat, and then eventually find a new youth pastor.
- Entice students with "exciting" programs and events with popular and charismatic guest speakers
- Claim that your church has many single people looking to get married (probably the worst solution ever).

What do all of these attempts have in common? They seek to trust in the plan and wisdom of men rather than the Word of God. Like Pharisees, they trust in their own understanding and nullify the Word of God with their traditions (Mark 7:13). Even though we may have good intentions in carrying out these solutions, we must first consider the potential long-term implications and messages we send when we use these methods. Are we offering temporary fleeting pleasures like the author of Ecclesiastes cautioned us against, or are we offering a genuine discipleship to the next generation today? We need to be encouraging them to carry the cross, deny one's self and, seek first the kingdom of God before all things.

A common argument then appears – "as long as they're in the church and potentially hearing the Gospel, it's better than them not coming to church at all!" However, we need to ask ourselves if there is any such model or like pattern found in scripture. I do not deny that many come to the Lord within the church, especially when it is preached intentionally, but when we take the time to investigate the early church, we see a pattern of the apostles going *out* into the world as Christ himself came down to this earth to reach us. As we study more in Acts 2:42-27, we see the faithfulness of the early Christians, praising God and having *favor among all the people* and it was the *Lord* who added to their number.

Another point to consider is whether we're trusting in a biblical model for the church, or have unknowingly depended on the traditions of men. If we cannot find biblical support in the way that we lead the church, then what else could it be? The only alternatives would be either a plan of man or a deception of Satan. Let us give heed to the apostle Peter's words in his first letter to the elders of the church, "Shepherd the flock of God that is among you, exercising oversight, not under compulsion, but willingly, as God would have you; not for shameful gain, but eagerly; not domineering over those in your charge, but being examples to the flock" (1 Peter 5:2-3).

Even though many of us may be older, let us never become so arrogant that we believe we have nothing else to learn (Proverbs 15:32).

Some of the most beautiful and difficult testimonies to hear are those of families immigrating to the United States. Back in 1965, immigration restrictions were released for Asian countries, leading to an influx of immigrants from the east coming to the west looking for a better life and possibilities. With every passing decade the number of immigrating families has almost doubled. The first wave of these immigrants consisted of unskilled laborers and many of them found themselves depending on relatives or others in the same circumstances to be able to survive in this new land. Many of them didn't know the language, and there were little to no government programs that would welcome them, teach them the basics, and send them on their merry way.

Enter the Korean church. There was a huge need and potentially a huge ministry in serving the migrating families. The church would act both as a hub and safe haven for those who were looking to find a better life here in the States. People could communicate easily in their native tongue, eat the foods that they ate in their home countries, and simply be themselves as opposed to the awkward foreigner in a new land. The church became a place not just for religious needs, but political and socio-economic needs as well.

Unfortunately, similar to the parable of the weeds (Matthew 13:24-30), many would often abuse the church's resources for their own gain. Perhaps churches were so happy to have opportunities with so many families coming that they were unable to remain focused on heavenly priorities. Sometimes when there is sudden explosive growth, many organizations including the church are ill-prepared to uphold consistent standards that they were able to when they were smaller. Additionally, some would be like wolves in sheep's clothing (Matthew 7:15) who would use influence and politics to gain authority. Being put in positions of eldership, they would promote unbiblical (albeit good intentioned) visions for the church. Let's remember Simon the Magician who saw the power of the Holy Spirit and believed, but sadly his heart was still in the wrong place, as he offered money to gain the ability to lay hands on others to give them the Holy Spirit (Acts 8). Is it possible that poor understandings, rather than poor intentions, have allowed those who are not qualified to be in leadership? If poor and false teachers have entered the Korean church over the generations, it figures that slowly but surely, the focus of many Korean American churches would be peace, community, financial comfort, honor titles and everything that the worldly Korean desires.

It is imperative that we as spiritual leaders who profess that we have been called by the Lord, ask ourselves whether or not we see remnants of these unbiblical practices and beliefs in our churches today. For example, has the Confucian practice of respecting one's elders taken priority over obedience to the Lord?[20] Some may argue that there is scriptural evidence for this in 1 Peter 5:5, where the younger are instructed to subject themselves to the elders, and this is correct to a certain extent. There are benefits in subjecting and humbling one's self to honor those who have more experience, however, believers also have the responsibility to be discerning and speak up against those who speak another gospel (Galatians 1:8-9) or when obedience is for the sake of men rather than God (Gal. 1:8-9; 1 Thess. 2:4). This is not a call for younger pastors to begin questioning all things that their senior leadership decides on, but

---

20 Some argue and point out that scripture supports the idea that we are to honor our elders and parents (Exodus 20:12; Ephesians 6:2). However, your loyalty to Christ takes higher precedence (Luke 14:26). For the sake of context, Jesus is not teaching us to hate our parents, but teaching us that our love for the Lord may cause division between us and our loved ones, including our parents.

rather a call for older leadership to reflect on the foundation of their ministries to determine whether it is built on the sand or on the rock.

Can we be honest with ourselves and ask if traditions of the culture take precedence over scriptural authority? If these things are happening in our church, it comes at the cost of the hearts of many people, particularly the upcoming generations as seen in the "silent exodus" phenomenon. We are actually promoting a church culture where many might come to the church physically, but their hearts are far from God (Matthew 15:8). We are in danger of committing the same sin as the Pharisees of Jesus' time by teaching the traditions of man as commandments of God (Matthew 15:9). As a result, many may perform the motions for a little while, especially if it allows them to be accepted into the community, but will end up leaving the church and being spiritually dead.

The other goal is for us to honestly reflect on whether or not our ministry styles are still applicable in today's generation and culture. As Paul became as a Jew to reach the Jews, and as a Gentile to reach the Gentiles, let us not assume that our old wineskins can carry the new wine that is needed for today's context in America, especially concerning our youth. Youth pastors such as myself understand and agree that the old traditional methods of Korea can be effective in discipling and running churches for the older generations, but are these methods still applicable and effective in the context of the upcoming generations? Not only that, but geographically speaking, our younger generations *do* grow up in a culture with different expectations and standards. Let's be careful not to be like the Pharisees and simply trust in our system to run the church, claiming that because we are the "sons of Abraham" (Matthew 3:9) that everything is settled. Rather we must seek a God who continues to make things new. The more we depend purely on liturgy and tradition, the less we embrace trusting in the Lord for things outside of our comfort zones.

Finally, as we dive deeper into the issue, we must be honest with ourselves. Does any type of criticism or even this type of *discussion* offend us? If that is the case, then is that not part of the problem? If we aren't willing to even communicate on these matters because we believe that we are correct, then are we not being foolish? A fool takes no pleasure in understanding, but only in expressing his opinion (Proverbs 18:2). Additionally, we must be careful because even though we believe that we are right, we can be blind to our own sins and flaws (Proverbs 18:17). Let us not forget that we as the spiritual leaders will be held to a higher standard (James 3:1). We are to shepherd the flock given to us, exercising oversight, not for shameful gain, not by domineering over them, but by being examples to the flock (1 Peter 5:2-4).

As a Korean myself, I can understand the difficulty of receiving criticism. Many Koreans today are not fond of confrontation because it brings us too close to admitting our wrongs and experiencing the shame that comes along with them. Still, we have to be careful not to let our pride force the next generation to pay the price for mediocre Christianity, or possibly cause them to completely abandon the faith altogether. Perhaps at the beginning of our ministries, we had good intentions and worked with those good intentions all these years, but the point of contention is not the intention of the older generations, it is whether the executions of our ministries are still effective in an ever-changing context.

There is a great need for an examination over our ministry structure and worldviews for the sake of the next generation and the current condition of their faith. As stated earlier, the issue of the "silent exodus" continues to this day, and for those who may stay in the church, they simply grow up in quiet bitterness and lukewarm faith. Although many are able to carry out the motions of worship within the church, most of them do not have the deep discipleship required to deal with the various issues of today. If we do not quickly shift our mentalities and methods on training up the next generation, I fear that they will be lost. The Church of Jesus Christ and all of her believers will last through eternity, but if we continue to hold onto antiquated practices that are grounded in traditions of men, then sadly many churches will eventually grow older and fade away.

Many of us know and recognize that through the narratives found in the Old Testament, we are actually seeing reflections of our lives, our struggles, and our sins. One particular reoccurring truth revealed there is that leadership always sets the tone for the rest of the people. Moses was a man of God who set a high godly standard on how the Israelites were to live and worship God. 1 Samuel shows the relationship between David and Saul, a man who chased after God's own heart, while Saul did what was right in his eyes. Clearly throughout the books of 1 Kings and 2 Kings, we see the depressing genealogy of kings who did wickedness in the eyes of God, leading to the suffering of the people, and ultimately resulting in Israel going into exile. Even in the New Testament, the apostle Paul repeatedly teaches us to imitate the elders and their faith (1 Cor. 11:1; 2 Thess. 3:7-9). The author of Hebrews in 13:7 tells us the same.

The message is quite clear: Leadership sets the tone for society, and that includes the culture of our churches. An overseer who loves the Word of God will most likely have a church who will respect it as well. A pastor who loves to reach out to the community will also have a church congregation who seeks to help their neighbors. This concept also applies to negative things. Leadership that focuses solely on liturgy and traditions of the church will have people who will do the same. A prosperity gospel teacher will have members who will love money and materialistic things. A false teacher will have followers who believe in lies. On and on, this truth is reaffirmed throughout history.

With that said, what is your current vision for the purpose of your church? Is there biblical support for your vision and do the actions and plans carried out also *follow* a biblical model?

Mark Dever, senior pastor at Capitol Hill Baptist Church in Washington, D. C. is very well known for his work over the purpose of church today. In short, he defines the purpose of God's church as follows:

"The church's mission and purpose lie at the heart of its nature, attributes, and marks; and right practices of

> *membership, polity, and discipline serve those purposes. To summarize, the proper ends for a local congregation's life and actions are the worship of God, the edification of the church, and the evangelization of the world.*
>
> *The church ultimately exists for the glory of God. Whether pursuing missions or evangelism, edifying one another through prayer and Bible study, encouraging growth in holiness, or assembling for public praise, prayer, and instruction, this one purpose prevails. The church is the unique instrument for bringing God such glory. According to the Bible, God's "intent was that now, through the church, the manifold wisdom of God should be made known to the rulers and authorities in the heavenly realms, according to his purpose which he accomplished in Christ Jesus our Lord." No lesser matters are at stake in the church than the promulgation of God's glory throughout his creation. As Charles Bridges expressed it, "The Church is the mirror, that reflects the whole effulgence of the Divine character. It is the grand scene, in which the perfections of Jehovah are displayed to the universe."*[21]

To summarize, the purpose of the church is to reflect the qualities and attributes of God the Father, the Son Jesus Christ, and the Holy Spirit to this world so that the end result will be the glory of God. The church carries out this duty through worship within the church as well as love and service outside the church (John 13:35; 1 John 4:20; Galatians 6:10; 1 Peter 2:5). The church does not mean a building or even a location, but a body of born-again believers coming together to celebrate what they have in Christ (Acts 2:42-47; Romans 12:1-8; 1 Corinthians 12). The highest priority that we have as followers of Christ is to carry out the Great Commission (Matthew 28:16-20).

---

21 Dever, A Theology for the Church, p. 809

Although I could go on and on concerning the purpose of the church, I write assuming that we who have gone through seminary or Bible school have a good grasp of what the church of our Lord is truly all about. This is not an issue of knowledge and understanding, this is an issue of whether within our hearts we trust and carry out the will of God concerning the purpose of His church. Even though we may have the rock and are saved, what are we building upon this foundation that has been given to us by Christ Jesus? In 1 Corinthians 3, the apostle Paul challenges his readers to consider the reality that Christ alone is the foundation. He also challenges them to consider what materials they are using to build upon this rock. We can offer what is truly precious – gold, silver, and gems – representing the works that are for our heavenly reward, or we can use wood, hay and straw – things that will not endure the fires that will truly test each man's work. "If anyone's work is burned up, he will suffer loss, though he himself will be saved, but only as through fire" (v. 15). Let us not make this tragic mistake as shepherds called by God in offering what is worthless to the Lord! We can only begin when we humble ourselves and are willing to seek obedience to our Lord's standard of ecclesiastical structure.

My eyes were opened on an overseas missions trip when I learned of the reality that some pastors in other countries still physically beat their wives. The reason for this was not because they were malicious sinners who wanted to hurt their wives, but rather that the concept was so ingrained in their culture that they believed nothing was wrong. You can then imagine the tears coming down their cheeks from their broken-heartedness when they were confronted by other overseas missionaries on their wrong behavior. They were literally blind to their sin because of their deep-rooted cultural beliefs!

One fascinating thing about the Korean community is our willingness to stand firm in our heritage. The biggest reason we stay so deeply rooted in our traditions is because we believe there is loyalty due to our elders and their ways. Many immigrating families typically hold firmly onto the culture of their motherland. We see the after-effects of this devotion to this day as many Korean services still sing hymns from the 1900s! None of these things are inherently wrong but may be holding us back from truly understanding the culture we live in today.

It is my plea to leaders today in the Korean American church, and really all churches of every ethnicity and tongue, to submit themselves to the authority of scripture in all things. As a Korean, I am proud of my heritage, my culture, the people and their hardiness, the food and yes even the traditions, but first and foremost my identity is founded in Christ. Therefore, my decisions, way of worship, and guidelines in leading the church are submitted to Christ alone, his Spirit and Word alone. When we let scripture dictate how we are to live our lives first, then I have no doubt that the Lord will use us in a way that still presents the beauty of our Korean heritage in our service. In his kingdom, there *will* be many tribes and nations praising his name, but the key focus will be on Christ, not our ethnicities. The worship and trust will be in our Lord, not our plans. We will celebrate being in the presence of our Creator, not our culture.

> *"Nobody is saved by belonging to a group when their individual heart is hard toward God."* —John Piper

Things to Consider

1. Do the responsibilities and methods of our original calling effectively apply to the current contemporary ministry needs?
2. Do we have a ministry vision that promotes discipleship in Christ or simply a safe haven for Korean immigrants?
3. Does scripture, or our culture and tradition, set the tone for our church?

CHAPTER 8
Are We Seeking First the Kingdom of God?

Earlier in this book, we discussed the influence of Confucianism and the Yangban government structure, where the foundation of Confucius teachings on the importance of academics, success, and family connections were the greatest and most respected priorities in life. Every time I study the culture of the Yangban whether through books or even through Korean dramas, I can't help but see the similarities to many churches today.

Examples of these similarities are seen in many of our discussions thus far, from the issues in the lack of communication between the older and younger generations, to expectations of loyalty with no questions asked in regards to their decisions.

One similarity that we haven't discussed is how elders and deacons are selected by their secular accomplishment, rather than biblical qualifications. Do we have a church that takes the time to investigate the biblical qualifications of someone nominated to be an elder or do we just honor them with a title due to their financial contribution and loyalty to the church?

I've had the privilege of participating in a few elder ordination interviews among other pastors who intentionally take the effort to pray, to interview, and to test the intentions, character, and qualifications of a nominee based on the standards of 1 Timothy 3. For some churches, the process can take up to 6 months! The interview process is often a grueling interrogation which doesn't just measure the intellectual level of the nominee, but their personal issues with sin, their family life, their doctrinal views, and even their philosophy of ministry. This may seem too legalistic for some, but I appreciate that there is a standard in choosing leaders who are "above reproach" (1 Timothy 3:2).

The Korean church must consider the fact that while secular qualifications are valuable, they are still secondary to the spiritual qualifications of leaders. It is heartbreaking to witness numerous elders stepping down due to conflict over worldly reasons (James 4:1-4), such as not receiving a certain title or position within the church. I've experienced a scenario where an elder candidate was rejected due to a lack of sufficient financial contribution to the church. Some who read these examples may find them outrageous and unbelievable and rightly so, but I know that many cannot deny that they have seen these instances happen.

I urge all leaders who have been called to shepherd the church to promote a culture where the biblical standard is the criteria in selecting our leaders. We must be careful not to fall into the sin of favoritism (James 2:1-13), where we are enamored by the money, the resources, and the potential financial blessing that comes from specific people. We also must be careful to avoid giving favoritism to our family members as the Yangban did; giving preference to and excusing those who are close to the senior leadership while raising unreasonable expectations of those who are not.

The church culture found in scripture is one that completely conflicts with the Yangban style of rule. The quality of a leader is not found in their accomplishments, or their services, but by their love for Christ and their desire for others to follow him. The goal in appointing leaders is not to be led by those who are qualified within the world, but to be led by those who have been called by Christ to lead others to Christ. As 1 Peter 5:1-3 says:

> "So I exhort the elders among you, as a fellow elder and a witness of the sufferings of Christ, as well as a partaker in the glory that is going to be revealed: shepherd the flock of God that is among you, exercising oversight, not under compulsion, but willingly, as God would have you; not for shameful gain, but eagerly; not domineering over those in your charge, but being examples to the flock."

We can assess our intentions with one question, but before I ask, let me offer a point of reflection. We are so good at deceiving ourselves and even justifying our behavior because of the distortions we create in our minds and hearts. I mention this because the Pharisees had this flaw, despite the warnings of our Lord. In Luke 7, Jesus points out the contradiction that the Pharisees make in their condemnation of both John the Baptist and Jesus himself. They judged John the Baptist for having a demon, despite the fact that he was not drinking wine and yet in the same manner, they judged Jesus when he was drinking with the tax-collectors. Luke 7 shows us that regardless of the truth that is in front of us, if the heart is not in the proper place, we will try to find every opposing argument because we are unwilling to admit our wrong. Nobody, including pastors, is safe from this temptation. Sometimes we run away from confession and repentance in the way that we lead our church by either hiding behind our authority and title (a la the Yangban), or covering it up with our spiritual resumes, using our contributions to excuse us from our misconduct. We shouldn't be like the Pharisees, making our tombstones shine while ignoring the dead bones inside, or making our cups clean on the outside but still holding greed and indulgence within, *especially* as first-generation Koreans!

With that said, will you ask yourselves dear pastors, to whom does your church belong? This question is answered not by our words, but by our actions, specifically the way that we actually run the church. If we still hold the mentality that because of our efforts and perhaps even the efforts of our previous generation, the current church we serve in belongs to us, then we *will* have a culture within our church where people are more focused on appeasing the senior pastor, following his methods and motions instead of God's Word. When you believe the church is yours and not the Lord's, that church's "success" is defined by the numbers, the budget, the programs offered, and the current approval rating from the congregation.

In contrast, a church that believes that Christ is the head (Colossians 1:18; Ephesians 1:22, 5:23) works toward a culture where success is not measured by what they have gained and can show off to others, but *what they are willing to give up for the kingdom of God.* This kind of church has respect and submission for the elders of the church due to their understanding that these men have been called specifically to oversee the souls of the church. (Hebrews 13:17). The congregation also has an understanding that they are people who serve Christ first in all things. When we follow a Yangban culture of running our church, then there is a risk that the priorities of the church are centralized on the issues of people, not the kingdom. Where the conflicts that your church experienced over spiritual and doctrinal disagreements (vision of the church, methods of evangelism, biblical curriculum, etc.), or were the conflicts due to arguments similar to those of Jesus' disciples concerning who was the greatest? (Luke 22:24-30)

I have seen church elders leave because they felt they were not being "recognized" for their work. I've seen families split within churches because they wanted certain positions and titles. I can't count the number of times there was drama in the choir groups because members were competing for the leading vocal part in the Christmas presentation. These things offer insight into the actual dreams and goals of the church congregation and have no biblical merit.

Let's contemplate even we introduce one another within the Korean context; the type of questions we begin with such as our family name, our background, where we grew up, what we currently do for a living, or what schools our children go to. Subliminally, we are assessing a person based on the cultural standards that have been ingrained in our history for many centuries. Can this type of culture be compatible with the discipleship-oriented culture that is found within scripture? Furthermore, can this type of Yangban structure provide what is necessary for the upcoming generation who face non-communal expectations? We cannot deny the fact that many of our older first-generation church members are slowly becoming the minority, and eventually the next generation will take charge of our churches. Are we preparing them to be leaders capable of navigating the everchanging societal (unbiblical) demands that the world puts on the church or are we preparing them to simply "maintain the church" and uphold the practices of the decade that we carried over from the motherland?

One concern that Korean American churches will soon face (if they haven't already) is the need to become a less-homogenous community. Although the previous generations needed to stick with their own people groups to survive in a foreign land, the upcoming generations will not have to do the same, nor are they likely to. With the increasing diversification of America, as well as the growing independence of our children who have been taught by society today to be blind to race and skin color, they *will* have non-Korean peers. They will also be hearing and discussing various worldviews that do not match up with the Korean mindset. Additionally, we will have youth groups which may start as a Korean body, the offspring of church members, but as they mature physically and spiritually, it is inevitable that non-Koreans will be invited.

Now before going any further, it is important to note that forced diversity has its share of cons, from external pressure to a belief that a diverse church would increase numbers and churches. By setting diversity as the highest goal, they shift their culture to become more "inviting" to other ethnicities. Sadly, although the intentions are commendable, and I do believe there has been some success in churches who pursue this route, the other effect has been a forced artificial acceptance. Even though the faces of the attendees are diverse, because the hearts have not been fully equipped or molded to love others with *differences in culture*, there will be conflict due to *the difference in culture*. At best there will be superficial relations with one another and at worst, there will be issues of racism and bias. When a group is not united in the mission of Christ, then they will be united in a plan of man. Eventually, the desires of each person will rise and clash with another, leading to division which is the exact opposite of what they intended.

We must take into consideration the needs of migrating families who *do* need a social safe haven to be able to survive in their new host country, and we cannot simply dismiss these needs for the sake of "diversity." This is not a call for Koreans or any other ethnicity to simply drop their cultural heritage and specific calling; this is a challenge for us, as the Korean church to consider the preparation and response required as the older generation passes away and the younger generation, a more diverse color-blind generation, takes charge.

Acts 2:47 shows us that because of the lifestyle of the early Christians, favor was earned in the eyes of the public, and the Lord added to their number. For the early believers who were deeply rooted in Jewish theology and the Mosaic culture of law and traditions, they were now faced with a new issue: Gentile Christians. These people had no understanding of the law and held many different worldviews and practices themselves. Those who are even somewhat versed in church history will know that various groups held various beliefs concerning the soul, the mind, and the body. We had the Judaizers who believed that salvation came through faith *and* by following the law, for which Paul the apostle rebuked Peter for falling to a false gospel (Galatians 2:11-21). We had ascetic groups who believed that any type of pleasure would be a sin and therefore forbade eating certain foods or even marrying (1 Timothy 4:3). On the other side of the spectrum, we had those who felt that the soul and the body were so distinct that anything done to the physical body would have no effect over the soul and the condition of salvation. Their salvation by a profession of faith alone made them believe they were justified to live free of restraint, even in sin because they were so secure in their salvation.

How would we respond to such situations? More importantly, how will our church congregation respond? In the face of the various new ways of living that the world will present to us, we will either respond in two ways: with the Gospel or with traditions of man. If we promote a faith that focuses more on the Korean way of doing things, then we can expect backlash from other cultures that hold different worldviews. We can also expect rebellion from our youth who spend the *majority* of their lives in environments among their peers which directly clash with our way of life. Remember, the next generation will follow the ones with whom they have close relationships, people who they trust, and people who will present to them an identity that they appreciate. Comare this to an environment where we simply pour burdens and expectations upon them, offering no explanation or even discussion, in every short moment that we have with them weekly. Which side do you honestly believe they will follow?

As we have covered these two hypothetical situations, our initial response gives us good insight into whether we believe the church belongs to us or to Christ. It is either the kingdom of God, or the kingdom of Korean men. For pastors who read this book and reflect on their years within ministry, I again plead for you to consider the that you have in setting the spiritual tone of your church. Let us remember that Christ himself warned the pharisees not to stick with their "old wineskins" trying to patch it up with a new patch, because the new wine would make them burst. (Matthew 9:14-17) John MacArthur, speaking on that particular passage puts it best, *"When I say the gospel is unique, I mean to say that it is incompatible with any and all other religious belief. It stands alone. The idea that the Christian gospel can mix with or blend with any other religious system in any way is absolutely wrong.* "If you can relate to having experienced any of these issues, I again urge you to consider going back to the purest gospel as the highest voice in leading a church and putting every Korean custom secondary to our Lord. We have both the calling and the authority of the Word to show that Christ is King, not our cultures.

Things to Consider
1. Does your current vision for your church promote a discipleship model where the next generation is able to take over?
2. What are the major issues that your church is dealing with today? Are they biblical or worldly issues?
3. How often do you communicate with your youth pastors in partnering together in resolving these issues?

CHAPTER 9
What is the Model for Your Church?

> *"...shepherd the flock of God that is among you, exercising oversight, not under compulsion, but willingly, as God would have you; not for shameful gain, but eagerly;"*
> *- 1 Peter 5:2*

We have spent the previous chapter assessing our visions for our church, so it may seem strange to ask what our model for church is, as they appear to be similar. One reflects the heart of leadership, while one reflects the actual execution. Intentions and competence are not the same thing! In this chapter, we will be covering a few more issues within the Korean American church and the biblical response to each one. This is not meant to be exhaustive, nor generalized to include all Korean American churches, but these are topics that I would consider important based on my personal experience and the experience of other younger pastors in the ministry, as well as years of discussion and counseling sessions with youth. I pray that these are not taken as criticism of your ministries, but rather as starting points to launch discussion with your second and third-generation pastors and members of your church. Perhaps these discussions could eventually lead to some reform in your models. No church will have all these problems and no church is free from any, but I pray you will find the suggested responses helpful for your church. Perhaps they will offer some insight into what the next generation is currently experiencing.

Leadership does not communicate with the younger generation; they just make demands.

Among my colleagues in the ministry, this is sadly the most common complaint that they have. Fortunately, there are some churches that have a great model for accountability and leadership that in my opinion follow the biblical model of having a plurality of elders. Sadly, there are still many churches that simply treat the youth, elementary, and praise and worship pastors as workers instead of elders over the church.

There are a few reasons this happens, specifically in the Korean American context. First, is the obvious language barrier. Many younger pastors who grew up in the states may not have had the privilege of learning their mother tongue. This of course does not disqualify them from ministry as long as they are able to lead the youth correctly, but it is a hurdle that does hinder clarity in communication, and creates awkwardness. Neither side wants to begin a discussion where they are incapable of saying the correct words. We must not let awkwardness or embarrassment be an obstacle to communication, but instead, humble ourselves and trust in the cause of Christ to do what it takes to speak and listen to our pastors.

Secondly, the aforementioned traditions of segregating ministries by age and by language only further reinforces stereotypes that youth pastors are the only ones who are capable of handling the youth and do not understand the intricacies of the real church. Sadly, because of the view that youth pastors are simply too young and inexperienced in the workings of the church, they are treated as such. Moreover, there is still a stigma in many Asian churches where elementary and youth ministry is viewed as a mere stepping stone into real ministry. A question that I and my colleagues in youth ministry often hear is, "have you ever thought of becoming a real pastor someday?" Disappointingly, this reflects some of the thoughts that people have about next-generation ministry.

Consider 1 Timothy 4:12, "Let no one despise you for your youth, but set the believers an example in speech, in conduct, in love, in faith, in purity." Paul encourages his student Timothy not to let the older men in his church discourage just him because they are older and have more experience. Paul wants him to understand that his ministry from the Lord is the ultimate source of value for his calling and his work and he is to prove this through his conduct. Although we do not know exactly how old Timothy was, it was likely that he was in his late 20s or early 30s. It's surprising to see such parallels between Timothy's case and the cause of many young and upcoming pastors in the Korean American church today and their issues with the older men of the church.

Let's also not forget the fact that the Lord has used many young men to accomplish his will in the past. Joseph, David, Daniel and his friends, even some of the disciples were young men used by the Lord to perform many examples of faith. There is a reason for this: The Lord uses the foolish to shame the wise and the weak things of the world to shame the strong (1 Cor. 1:27). The Lord uses the weaker vessels in life so that the glory and trust goes to Him and not the works and wisdom of men. Sometimes, we as Koreans who are hardworking achievers have the tendency to boast about our works and accomplishments. Because of the sacrifices and long hours that we have invested into our business or churches, there is the temptation to believe that we deserve the credit. The risk of this belief however is the tendency to forget about the Lord, to become less trusting of those who are seemingly unqualified in our eyes, and to ultimately promote the idea that only the qualified are capable of serving the Lord.

Let's boycott the inapplicable Confucian concepts that do nothing to help our ministries in a western context, and instead, obey scripture's standard of how to treat our fellow lay leaders. Let's stop seeing the younger pastor as a worker who can be replaced, but rather as fellow *elders* who oversee such a valuable aspect of your church: the next generation.

Some practical things to work towards:

Even if you disagree, give your younger pastors a chance to speak – Even though our culture has inherited the Confucian practice of respecting one's elders, even though they may be wrong, this does not exactly match what scripture says. Throughout Proverbs, there is a repeated theme of foolishness not stemming from ignorance, but rather from an unwillingness to listen and receive correction. To be blunt, it is very arrogant of anyone to claim that their way is 100% correct. 1 John 1:8 is very clear: "if we say we have no sin, we deceive ourselves and the truth is not in us." The goal of our ministry is not to carry out our beliefs, but scriptural truth. We must be very careful not to commit the same mistakes as the Pharisees. Honestly ask yourself, "When was the last time that I admitted my wrongs to my pastors?" I'm not talking about to your close friends or your spouse. I'm talking about those you serve within ministry. Humility is one of the greater attributes of a good leader.

As we grow older, we can remain focused on our specific callings for some time, and we must understand that we may have missed some of the tools and knowledge in adapting to the everchanging cultures we live in. Consider the speed of our technological advances even within the past decade. There are still many who don't fully know how to use a computer today while children seemingly know all the ins and outs of tablets. This is why the younger youth pastor is a blessing. I strongly believe that the Lord *has* called many of them because they have been gifted to relate with the upcoming generations. Whether it's contemporary examples in their sermons, applicable humor, or even slang, these men have been blessed to be able to understand and empathize with the youth of today.

Let's work towards accepting the idea that today's youth pastors are able to understand the trends of the current adolescent generation which give them an edge in reaching out to our youth. Sometimes, the solutions that they offer *will* clash with our beliefs and even challenge us to break away from our comfort zones of honor and respect. Let's remind ourselves that many of our second-generation pastors study and train in American schools which naturally teach many American church strategies and visions. This isn't without benefit however, as American seminaries are among the best in understanding and responding to the trends that happen in western culture. Many conservative seminaries are probably the most biblically-grounded schools in the entire country and as a result, hold a higher priority toward the biblical standard and less on the cultural expectation. If our youth pastors have such strong biblical support which ultimately pushes them toward discipling youth into following Christ more deeply, who are we to question the Word of God? We should be coming alongside these lay leaders who have been called by the Lord to reach the next generation. Pray that nothing hinders the work of our Lord regardless of the vessel he chooses to use. This is a challenge for us to trust not in the youth pastor, but in the Spirit of the Lord working through those he has called.

Find ways to communicate with your pastors – If there is a massive language barrier, then find an interpreter. Use Google translate if you have to. The key is having a desire to communicate with one another. Like youth, younger pastors will appreciate feeling respected and cared for. I strongly believe that despite a Korean/English language barrier, two solid men of God who love Christ can still communicate the vision of a church by simply opening up a Bible and pointing to the appropriate verses. Remember that communication is a two-way street. Meetings should not be times where you tell your "workers" what to do, they are be times to hear the concerns and happenings of other ministries in your church.

Perhaps the simplest but most often forgotten way to communicate with your pastors is to pray over them. Even if it is in Korean and they cannot understand everything, take the effort to pray over them in person. Don't just pray for the ministry that they do, but pray over their personal and spiritual needs. The more you treat them as an individual, which is something that is expected in the western culture, the more you will find a happy and joyful worker ready to fight for you.

Protect your pastors – 1 Timothy 5:19 sets a very healthy guideline in terms of how we should take care of our pastors. "Do not admit a charge against an elder except on the evidence of two or three witnesses." There is a reason for this and I believe many pastors already know it. Leaders are often put into situations where they will have to make difficult decisions. These difficult decisions often make certain people happy while making others disappointed, or even angry. Furthermore, selfishness and sin can cause people to make unwarranted accusations against pastors. Young pastors need the same amount of protection and support as does anyone in a leadership position. This is not to say that youth pastors remained untouched from scandals, but when we consider the fact that there are members who complain about our decisions, there will also be members of the church who will gossip and slander other pastors. I am not suggesting a generalized answer for this topic, but I do want to encourage pastors to make sure that they are giving other pastors a say when issues appear.

One example I can offer is when a younger pastor seemingly offends an "older person", which includes parents. For Korean pastors who give preference to culture in honoring our elders, oftentimes they will not give an ear to the statements of the pastor, even if they are biblically correct! You can imagine the frustration that comes in these scenarios because even though the intention of the youth pastor was to follow scripture, he instead gets reprimanded. It sends a confusing message! Do not forget the message in James 2 where the apostle warns against the sin of favoritism. I encourage senior pastors today not to fall back on traditions, or to simply favor the older due to complacency in cultural habits, but to treat each case fairly and biblically.

Remember to make followers of Christ, not copies of you.

One adage that exists in Korean churches today is that the pastor is to sacrifice everything for the sake of ministry. Whether its' sacrificing sleep by coming to morning prayer daily, or sacrificing time with their families because of the amount of work that naturally comes with the calling, or even taking an unofficial oath to live impoverished lives to "set an example of humility" towards the congregation.

Although these may seem like honorable motives, they aren't necessarily biblical ones. I've seen pastors never taking a sabbath for themselves because of the ministry despite the fact that it is direct disobedience to Exodus 20:8-11 and Mark 2:27. We should also consider the narrative of Mary and Martha, where Martha was utterly frustrated at her sister for not helping her prepare for dinner. In Martha's eyes, she could not believe her sister had the audacity of just sitting at the feet of Jesus, listening to him speak while she toiled away by herself. Jesus gently rebuked Martha, letting her know that there were more important things to consider.

The reason why I share these points is to remind and challenge older pastors today as to their intentions in leading the church and in regard to how they are raising up leaders for the next generation. Is your intention to raise up gospel-centered disciples who want to teach and obey everything that Christ has taught us (Matthew 28:19-20)? Or are we in danger of traveling across sea and land to create a proselyte of hell (Matthew 23:15)? Some leaders that I have worked with constantly refer to themselves and their past experiences more than what scripture states. Experiences are great tools to promote biblical truth, but when they alone are used as the guideline towards running the church, then that's an issue. Just because you have experienced the positives and negatives of a certain method doesn't necessarily mean it will apply in all future scenarios. Would it be correct to demand and expect a dramatic conversion experience from someone to prove that they actually came to the Lord? It would be ridiculous to have such a standard. In the same manner, it would be incorrect to claim that a certain genre of Christian music is "more holy" simply based on your preference alone.

Although we may have many positive motives, we must also entrust people to the Lord, and recognize that discipleship does not mean creating someone who is skilled, equipped, and believes in the same things we do. Let us remember the fact that not everyone in the church is an eye or a nose (1 Corinthians 12:17-20). Instead let's appreciate that the Lord can be served in a variety of manners. To be clear, this is no suggestion that we distort, dilute, or alter the gospel truth in any shape or form, but to point out that people *can* be gifted in different ways, even with different theological opinions, and yet still truly and genuinely love the Lord. Although there are definitely similar experiences in life that we can share to help encourage and guide others, we must allow these to create a dependence on Christ instead of a dependence on you. Our loyalty and submission to an authority-oriented culture makes this difficult for some, and in no way am I insisting mutiny against leaders we disagree with, but we as shepherds will be more harshly judged (James 3:1) and we who are in leadership positions serve a greater master, Christ Jesus (Ephesians 6:9).

It is sad when I hear stories of pastors who were reprimanded by older pastors because they took a Sunday off to take care of their sick child and/or spouse, or when younger pastors burn out and leave the ministry because of the amount of work and unreasonable expectations piled upon them with the reasoning of "that's how it's been done." Just because we have come to a certain conclusion doesn't necessarily mean it will apply to everyone else, especially if there is no scripture to back it up. Let's work toward a plurality of elders which *includes* the younger generation and an environment that supports and encourages one another while keeping accountability and transparency. If we have entrusted the youth ministry to these men, shall we not also consider their opinions and insights on the latest issues of the next generation? The upcoming generation of pastors are not workers to be used, but leaders who will be used by God to lead His church tomorrow. Are we promoting that or hindering that with our ministry styles?

What is your Model for Growth and Outreach?

Just within the recent generation, American Christianity went through a phase known as the "seeker-friendly church" system. Within this structure, the main goal was to appeal to as many non-believers as possible by catering to their needs and desires. Churches who followed this model would do whatever it took to dismiss the "outdated" concept and image of church, and introduce exciting settings for praise, pastors who were charismatic and uplifting, and events that would promote "community." There have been examples of churches where the first 100 attendees for a certain Sunday would receive a free iPod. As long as people were within the church building and were able to hear the Gospel, it would be considered a success.

This investment came with both good and bad news. The good news was that through this model, people *did* come to the Lord. People who had never heard the gospel attribute their salvation to the fact that the church was willing to do what it took to simply share the life-giving message of Jesus Christ. The bad news however, was that although they entered church doors, many would also leave. Additionally, those who stayed often developed a very shallow Christian faith, similar to some in the parable of the sower. If the church ceased to be entertaining, they would leave. If the children's ministry was insufficient or disagreed with the worldviews of the parents, they would leave. Ultimately this type of model, with some exceptions, raised up a generation of consumer Christians instead of servant-minded Christians, where one seeks to be served rather than to serve. Bible-believing pastors understand that the Christian life is one of sacrifice and cost. (Matthew 7:13-14; 8:18-22; 10:22; et al.)

Are Korean churches in danger of this consumer model or other seemingly biblical models with hidden repercussions? Interestingly enough, there are subtle ways that this seeker-friendly mentality can appear. Do we currently hold a church culture that furthers this cycle of simply holding firmly onto Korean traditions under the guise of honoring our elders at the cost of a gospel-centered church?

Let's reflect on some common seeker-friendly church models as we critique our own ministries:

Trusting in the Latest Fad – Whether it is a popular book, a famous Christian speaker, or even a VBS program, does it seem like we are always searching for the next new thing to keep our people excited? What happens when the excitement dies down or the resources become scarce? Will your church members stay faithful? Does your current program seek to disciple people as unique individuals or are you more concerned about the numbers?

Copying Another Church Model? – It can be unnerving when you have invested in your ministry for decades and yet cannot seem to grow as much as that church down the street. The temptation to simply follow their model can exist. This should be dealt with on a case-by-case basis, but some questions to consider are: Have we taken into consideration the specific needs that our congregation has that the other church does not (social, financial, age, etc.)? Are you being content and faithful to what the Lord has given to you, knowing that to some he gives a lot and to others he gives a little? Is the success of the other church measured by numbers or by actual spiritual growth? What is your true motivation in desiring a larger church? In understanding that there are some general patterns within the church, is it possible that your current congregation has been gifted to fulfill another need and ministry within the same region?

As touched upon in previous points, the style of ministry that we currently hold stems from the desires of our hearts. We must humbly ask ourselves and seek accountability (even with western leaders) concerning how we personally define success within the church and attest to biblical support.

As LifeWay Christian Resources president and CEO, Thom Rainer says, *"When the preferences of the church members are greater than their passion for the Gospel, the church is dying."*

Selection of Leadership and Teachers

> *"Not many of you should become teachers, my brothers, for you know that we who teach will be judged with greater strictness."* - James 3:1

> *"The saying is trustworthy: If anyone aspires to the office of overseer, he desires a noble task."* - 1 Timothy 3:1

One thing is clear throughout scripture: Our Lord takes his name seriously. The third commandment is not a mere suggestion in keeping our words clean, but it is a reminder of how even the name of our Lord is both a description and an attribute. The Israelites, being given the calling of God's chosen people, were called to live a certain life to uphold and reflect the testimony of our Lord. The same goes for Christians today where even the title "Christian" conveys that this person is a follower of Christ or a reflection of Christ. Now let's consider the higher standard placed upon spiritual leaders. In one sense, usually influenced by your denomination, some people believe that all Christians are on a certain level; "pastors" due to 1 Peter 2:9. Others take a stricter approach, stating that only pastors should be able to hold communion and perform baptism. Regardless of your view, I believe both sides will agree that only some have been gifted to teach and lead (1 Corinthians 12:28) and selection of these leaders should be taken seriously (1 Timothy 3).

As we have investigated how the Yangban mentality has infiltrated our church governments, especially within Asian American churches, it is especially important for us to assess our current leadership selection process. Do we hold a biblical model in hiring and ordaining elders within our church or have we been influenced by other factors such as politics and even money? Do we place a higher trust in academic degrees while overlooking important matters such as spiritual character and integrity?

To answer these questions, we can simply observe our intentions in our current leadership selection process. For example, if we view youth ministry, merely as a "side ministry" then the standards we hold in choosing leaders will be mediocre at best. Perhaps we believe that as long as they have the biblical knowledge to teach what is necessary and the skillset to carry out the motions of ministry, they will be sufficient for the position. Are elders ordained for their ability to disciple others in the Word through modeling as well as teaching, or are they elected simply by the amount of political and financial influence they have within the church?

As discussed earlier in this book, we have observed that academic capability alone is insufficient in regards to leading any form of ministry.[22] People who depend strictly on knowledge can still lack empathy towards others, become legalistic in their ministry style, and be absent in character. Throughout this text I have expressed the need for discipleship and relationship especially within the rising generations. Any ministry style where they are simply told what to do is exactly the reason why many youth are leaving our churches today. In our interview processes, what *are* the first qualities that we look for? Speaking as a Korean, I still have the tendency to ask the following questions when meeting new people: Where are you from? What school did you go to? What do you do for a living? What do your parents do? These may touch upon the characteristics of a godly leader, but the question still stands as to whether or not we're seeking people based on our cultural standard or a biblical standard. Let's consider the following questions to ask within an interview:

- How do you deal with conflict, especially within leadership?
- How do you deal with criticism?
- Can you give examples of work you performed that you weren't necessarily passionate about, but that was necessary for the ministry?

---

[22] Chapter 4

✦ Do you have a group of people who keep you accountable and encouraged?

✦ How much time do you invest in learning?

Hopefully we can see that the pattern of these questions seek to delve into their character – how they respond in certain circumstances, and how they really view their philosophy of ministry. These types of inquiries do not simply test their knowledge, but their character. Our next chapter goes into more detail about the interview process, but to put it bluntly, we will either hire leaders who will work toward gospel-centered causes or simply to fulfill the work and obligations that naturally come within a Korean American church. The type of leader that you select for your church is a reflection of what you desire for your church.

Let's consider another growing issue that the Korean American church must deal with today: the need for background checks. I am amazed at the lack of any formal background checks that are done for teachers and leaders who are elected to teach children. Perhaps due to the shame and honor culture that does not try to probe further than what is required, we feel that there is no need to do such a thing. Perhaps because the testimony and suggestion of an elder or church member holding the higher authority causes us to merely forego such matters due to our need for submissiveness. Many people have hidden pasts, and legally should not be near our children. What have we done to adapt to these changing dangers?

Any position of service within the church, ranging from the Sunday School teacher to the deacon who leads the bus-driving ministry is a position of influence. Are we simply seeking to fill the position to look good before men, or to possibly boast in the fact that our church has this many pastors and members, all at the cost of genuine faith and discipleship? Do we not see the potential risks involved when we offer titles to those who do not fulfill the standard? Do we risk ruining the testimony of Christ by giving biblically-unqualified people the banner to hold when they themselves bear bad fruit? This is not a demand for spiritual perfection, but as Peter quotes our Lord, "Be holy, because I am holy." It is a reflection of whether or not they truly love the Lord, understand the gospel clearly (1 Timothy 3:9), and first seek the kingdom of God in all that they do. The priority should not be simply "filling in the empty position" but being thankful and content in all circumstances and seeing how it challenges us to trust in the Lord. Perhaps the lack of a formal youth pastor is a situation for parents to step up and lead the next generation. Perhaps the lack of a guitarist for your praise team is simply a reminder of the true reason for worship. When we focus so much on simply filling the need, we can forget the truly important matters.

Busyness ≠ Faithfulness

With exceptions here and there, the title that Koreans hold as the "model minority" is definitely warranted. Throughout my years in the Korean community, my respect for my people will never waver in terms of the amount of work, effort, and endurance they demonstrate in their lives. Whether it's working long hours through the week for numerous decades at the same menial labor job. This work ethic is also found within the Korean American church, where pastors seemingly run on no sleep as they take care of their pastoral responsibilities. Events such as "revival nights", coffee house fundraisers, and typical holiday programs are common within many Korean churches today as they offer an opportunity for fellowship and joint worship within the entire church.

Work and busyness, as well as programs are not innately sinful in and of themselves, but as scripture tells us, at times they do come at a cost. Let's consider the narrative of Martha and Mary once again (Luke 10:38-42). Martha was frustrated because her sister was not helping her prepare dinner, and was simply sitting at the feet of Jesus listening to his teachings. It got to the point where Martha demanded Jesus to scold her sister for not helping. But Christ surprises Martha by challenging her to consider her actual priorities. Although her work in preparation is not condemned, he gently points out to her that time spent with him is much more valuable than any dinner.

As the famous Christian preacher Adrian Rogers once said, "If Satan can't make you bad, he'll make you busy." We can fall into that trap of simply equating a full schedule with a faithful Christian life. Similar to how Korean people assess a person through their school, degree, and their current work, that same mentality can permeate our church culture as well. Let's examine some of the repercussions of a church culture that focuses on busyness.

The Risk of Burnout – "The Sabbath was made for man, not man for the Sabbath" (Mark 2:27). Even before the Mosaic law, the Lord set one day of the week as a day of rest and remembrance of the Lord. In their concern of upholding the laws of the Sabbath, the Pharisees had missed the original purpose. Do we find ourselves falling into the same trap? When we factor in our Korean endurance and pursuit of excellence, has it come at the cost of taking a consistent sabbath? Scripture is also very clear that our Lord took time away from people to pray to our Heavenly Father. And the greatest danger of ignoring a sabbath is the slow but sure burnout in which our ministry is no longer a joyful calling, but merely a job in which we "maintain", not lead, our church.

Not only that, the benefits of resting on the sabbath or on a sabbatical allows us to reflect on our relationship with and calling from the Lord. It is a prime time for many pastors to use this free time to study more and become more aware of the latest trends and issues happening within the church today.

The Sacrifice of Family – A ministry defined by busyness is one that brings great risk to the health of the family. Paul is very clear in his letter to Timothy that an elder, "must manage his own household well, with all dignity keeping his children submissive" (1 Timothy 3:4), and also provide for his relatives (v. 5:8). Speaking as a pastor myself, the temptation to simply *do* more exists. Because when we see a need, naturally our pastor's heart seeks to fulfill that need. However, the calling of the pastor is secondary to the calling of a father and husband. A simple Google search can show us the numerous examples of families splitting up and in turmoil due to the burdens of ministry. This is particularly more difficult for our wives who not only have to live a lifestyle where their husband is technically on call 24/7 but also bear the other burdens that typically come with being a pastor's wife.

I believe Mark Dever hits the mark again in his book, *Understanding Church Leadership*, "[My] congregation can get another pastor, but my children cannot get another father, or my wife another husband."[23]

When we remember that the church belongs to the Lord and not us, that'll give us the humility to step down when necessary and hand the reins over to someone else as we take care of our responsibilities as fathers and husbands.

Events and Programs Do Not Disciple – Although I firmly believe that church events and programs have their place, especially if they are evangelical in nature, let us take caution that the quality of the event is the greatest priority. Red flags that we need to watch out for:

- ✦ When people argue over non-gospel oriented matters that it creates a sufficient distraction from the main purpose.
- ✦ When the amount of work and money expended in one area of church ministry is disproportionate to other ministries in the church such as missions, outreach, and inreach.
- ✦ When there is excitement and "faithfulness" during the season of these events but a lack of joy throughout the rest of the year.

Another point to consider is that programs, especially larger ones, can potentially push the church away from a discipleship-oriented culture. People become focused on the motions of worship and "finishing the job" rather than the true purpose of the church. It's easy to fall into the trap of believing that the success or failure of the event determines a person's success or failure as a believer! The nature of programs

---

23 Pg. 27

and events treat our members as workers rather than individuals. Let's follow the model of 1 Corinthians 12 and consider all parts of the body, whether big or small, honorable. Let's work towards a culture that seeks to train and equip believers to mature in faith, not being deceived, and working together to love one another (Ephesians 4:12-16).

It is our nature as Koreans to faithfully serve the Lord amidst any hardships that come, but let us not be deceived into thinking that the quantity of our works determines our goodness in the eyes of our Lord. The greatest danger from a culture of busyness is the risk of sending the message that faithfulness is measured by the number of your works. Although mature believers may be capable of guarding their hearts from a work-based faith, what about new believers and visitors? When we consider the fearful words of Matthew 7:21-23, many who attend church faithfully can still make the tragic mistake of believing their faithfulness is based on their works, not faith. Let's boycott that type of culture!

Final Note: There are many good books[24] on setting healthy boundaries. For the sake of our families, our ministries and even our own personal relationship with the Lord, let us stop defining faithfulness through our works.

The Need for Confrontation

One final matter that I feel warrants discussion is how church discipline and biblical counseling fits into the Korean church context. Understandably, within a culture that holds both an honor-shame system and a hierarchy based on age and seniority, the actual act of confrontation may be extremely difficult.

Scripture is very clear on the need for discipline within the church. Matthew 18 shows us the process in confronting a brother who has sinned against us. First there is a personal confrontation over the

---

24 *Boundaries* – Henry Cloud – ISBN – 0310351804

    Margin: Restoring Emotional, Physical, Financial and Time Reserves – Richard Swenson – ISBN – 1576836827

    Zeal without Burnout - Christopher Ash – ISBN – 1784980218

matter, then an introduction to a mediator if the first step is unsuccessful. Then the matter is brought to the attention of the church; a failure to repent within that scenario is grounds for excommunication from fellowship. 1 Corinthians 5 shows us another example of a person who professed to be a believer but was committing a sin that even the pagans found abominable. Paul is clear, with what was most likely the third warning, that the church of Corinth was to expel this person from the congregation for the sake of the sanctity of the church. The testimony of Christ had higher priority than the acceptance that the Corinthians most likely gave to this man.

The difficultly appears when the need for church discipline applies to an elder. Because of our natural response to show respect and honor to those older than us, the concept of disciplining someone older may be outrageous to many traditional Koreans. This is the crossroads which we pastors forced to choose between honoring elders or following the Word of God. This is something that we must prayerfully reflect on in terms of what holds the highest priority in our hearts and beliefs. This can vary in difficulty depending on who is actually involved. I can only imagine the amount of prayer that would be involved in disciplining an actual overseer/pastor of a church who has been there for many years. Although various opinions can be offered concerning this topic, the Holy Spirit can give us the proper direction and conviction necessary. As scripture shows us, a "little leaven leavens the entire lump" (1 Corinthians 5:6). The more we fear the expectations and traditions of men, the more the biblical integrity of our church is tarnished.

Furthermore, let us never allow the risk of shame to prevent us from offering necessary help for those who are in actual need. I speak specifically to the need of professional counseling for many families today. Those who are deeply invested in their church know of the many broken homes from which our church members come. Despite the fact that Koreans hold the "model-minority" title, there are numerous instances of broken marriages, abusive parents, drug use, and involvement with gangs among our people. The reality is, some legitimately require professional counseling. Will we refuse to point our church members to professional help simply because we do not want to shame them? As the Lord was counter-cultural in his ministry, challenging the norms and beliefs that the religious leaders and people had at the time, let us too break free from some of our cultural bonds which prevent people in need from getting actual help.

As we have gone over these issues within the Korean American church today, it is my prayer that we never receive them as criticism, but as advocacy. My purpose is to simply raise awareness of certain issues that exist in our ministries that may have gone unnoticed due to misunderstandings, a lack of knowledge, or perhaps even our unwillingness to change. Will we continue to allow our non-Christian, cultural origins to dictate how we shepherd our churches, or will we trust in the Lord and let his Word be the ultimate authority, allowing him to do the work through us? May the love of our Lord, for his people, and obedience to his Word be the everlasting vision for all of our ministries today and the generations to come. This begins with you, the leadership. May you fear God and keep his commandments, more than any fear of man and man-made rules. Truly, may the grace of our Lord Jesus Christ, the love of our Heavenly Father, and the fellowship of the Holy Spirit guide our hearts for his glory alone.

CHAPTER 10
The Real Purpose of Youth Ministry

"Likewise, urge the younger men to be self-controlled."
- Titus 2:6

I was a depressed child back in high school. Although I was blessed to have good friends, I didn't look forward to going home after school. My parents would often argue and there was always that anxiety of whether everything was going to be alright that night. School wasn't that much better either. I did pretty well academically; I was a very different child who didn't follow popular beliefs and trends. I (fortunately) thought that drinking and the party scene was foolish and a waste of my time. I hated materialism and hated people who were materialistic, and I hated Korean people.

That is not a typo. I did not like Koreans because I grew up in America most of my life and enjoyed the aspects of freedom and individuality. I hated the fact that all these Korean students came to my school, demanding respect because I was their junior and they, my senior. I also hated the fact that they seemed so homogenous! They would wear the same clothes and identical hairstyles, which clashed with my western style of uniqueness.

So, all in all, because of a tense home environment, dealing with people I didn't like at school, and holding countercultural beliefs without any real understanding of why, I led a pretty miserable life.

God revealed to me years later the reason why I went through a difficult adolescence: to be a youth pastor who would be able to sympathize with the younger generation. Because of my difficult years as a teen, I am better able to relate to many students who go through similar issues. Because of this, I still have ongoing relationships with my former students, who continue to meet with me and visit me till this day.

I share this about myself to prove a point: **There are many good gospel-centered youth pastors who are on your side.**

I say good, not perfect, because there *are* poor ones out there. People who shouldn't be anywhere near youth ministry. I have seen many who have entered ministry simply because there was nothing else to do, and then sadly use youth ministry merely as a stepping stone to the next position. Sadly, because when this occurs, it is the students who suffer spiritually.

I say gospel-centered because youth pastors are to be measured by their love and obedience towards Christ. Their skillset and degrees should be byproducts of their relationship with the Lord, not the first standard. They should understand that the problems with people are due to the heart and only the gospel of Jesus Christ can truly change the heart of teens!

Let's test our worldviews: What do *you* believe is the purpose of youth ministry? Why do you believe your response is correct?

Over the years, even though they may not say it directly, you can get a good sense of what people think youth ministry should be. Some still treat it as a Christian baby-sitting service while others treat it as a place where you can drop your youth off to transform them into well-behaved Christians. We also cannot deny the fact that some parents believe youth ministry should be a place to grow academically, network, and build up their child's extra-curricular resume.

If you doubt this, simply observe the major complaints parents have about youth ministry and church activities they allow their child to attend. This includes complaints about fun social events, the lack of programs they can add to their child's college application, and the like. It is unfortunate that many of the against youth ministry are consumer-driven and have little gospel influence. The final straw which causes many youth pastors to leave the ministry due to burnout or broken hearts, is the fact that many will blame the youth pastor for the lack of "success" of the ministry. Success that is defined by their eyes and not according to scripture.

As a youth pastor for 10 years, it is my ongoing desire that the Korean American church will embrace youth ministry for what it really is meant to be – a ministry that will raise disciples of Christ who obey his commandments (John 14:15) and teach others to do the same (Matthew 28:20). Fortunately, there are a growing number of churches today that work toward a Gospel-centered youth ministry that is discipleship oriented and partners (rather than competes) with parents in raising up youth in the ways of the Lord.

To offer some insight into the real purpose of youth ministry, let's take a look at the origin and history of where it all began. Back in the mid-1900s, Christians recognized that there was a need for introducing the Gospel and Christ to teenagers within public schools. Their purpose was to care for these youth who most likely had needs, especially behavioral ones, and sought to connect them with adults who could mentor and disciple them. As these ministries exploded in popularity, these groups would begin actively pursuing unsaved teenagers by promoting rallies and clubs. Soon thereafter, the growth of student groups led to the need for the "youth pastor", someone who could dedicate themselves full time to carrying out these responsibilities.

There were some negative repercussions from these well-intentioned programs. Students who originally worshipped with the older generation in intergenerational worship slowly segregated into their own worship services. The blessings of being in close proximity to an older mentor and having someone to imitate was lost. To make matters worse, as youth ministry became normalized, competing forms of entertainment such as TV, video games, and movies contributed to shallow and consumer-driven services. No longer were students being challenged to grow in biblical knowledge, to endure hardships, or to serve one another, but rather they expected things to be done for them. If church wasn't entertaining enough, they'd either find another church or leave the faith entirely.

Does this sound familiar? Just a few generations ago, the Korean church in America was a sapling that had to endure the struggles of migrating into a new country. They learned the language and culture, found financial, emotional, and spiritual stability. It ten comes as no surprise that the Korean church would follow what seemed popular and appropriate to expand their churches, garnering more resources to be able to help serve the ongoing influx of migrating Koreans to this country. When we look at the apparent positives of youth ministries and all the glamour that comes with it, we have fallen the trap of believing this pseudo-Christianity is the future. Furthermore, since excitement and entertainment *do* bring initial temporary success, we have misinterpreted that as success and blessings from God, and have doubled down on these methods.

In this entire book, this is perhaps my greatest plea to first-generation Korean pastors: Please do not trust in a youth ministry that seeks to entertain the youth with a little bit of Christianity here and there. This is not real Christianity and you are actually contributing to the issue of students leaving the church upon entering college.

Let us break free from comfortable trends and the traditions that have been passed down and challenge ourselves to seek the biblical guidelines for how to run the church, especially youth ministry. Let's work toward a generation where parents have strong, spiritually-founded relationships with their child, and children possess integrity and a clear moral compass. Let's work toward raising a generation of genuine believers who seek to bear much fruit and produce thirty, sixty, and a hundred more disciples. Let us reject our pride and actually seek the answer. Let us never make our misinterpretation of Christianity and assumptions of how life should be the reason why our youth actually turn out to be something entirely different from what we wanted them to become.

Discipleship

So, you might be wondering, what *is* and *should be* the purpose of youth ministry?

The answer is both simple and complicated.

Complicated because as different regions of the world have different blessings and needs, youth ministry will similarly have different focuses based on the youth that attend. Some might have a higher need to mentor students who don't have strong parental figures and come from broken families. Others may simply need more teachers to equip parents to understand the importance of discipleship and supplement biblical knowledge to teens.

Regardless of the unique needs of each youth ministry, they all point back to the simple answer: We are to raise disciples of Christ, teaching them to obey everything that he has taught us (Matthew 28:19-20).

The key to youth ministry is not based on what we believe nor what the youth believe to be the best for themselves. What our Lord says is best, and we know this through what scripture says. Scripture has a *lot* to say about our purpose here on earth. Romans 11:36 speaks about how all glory belongs to the Lord. 1 Corinthians 6:20 and 10:31 speaks about how we were bought with a price, Christ Jesus, so therefore we are to honor him with our bodies. There are numerous chapters in the Psalms that speak about our purpose and relationship with the Lord. Psalm 86 speaks about our utter need to be with God. Psalm 16 speaks about how he is our direction. On and on scripture speaks about man's need for God as a Father, a shepherd, a savior, and our King.

If this is true for all mankind, does that not include our own children as well? Contrary to popular belief and our cultural lens, our youth *are* capable of understanding the complexities of the Christian faith. We should no longer believe that our children must reach a certain age of understanding to introduce them to the Christian faith, but from birth we should dedicate our time to teaching them and training them up in godly ways. The only way that this will be accomplished is when we entrust our youth to the Lord, through obedience to His word.

Christian writer A.W. Tozer once said, "Your worship of God is no higher than your understanding of him", which means the more you know about God, all of his attributes and his works, the better and more genuine your worship of God becomes. If we still believe that God is just an old grandfather figure sitting in the clouds all day looking down upon us, then there is little motivation to give praise to Him. However, when we recognize that He is our savior, we offer Him thanks. When we truly recognize that He is our creator, we give Him praise and attention. When we recognize His holiness, we give him our awe and reverence. This is one of the most important aspects in Christian maturity, for understanding who we are in the presence of God encourages us to respond with worship. When our children see in us a sincere love for the Lord and a desire to worship him, this can have a positive influence on the growth of their own faith.

"Fathers, do not provoke your children to anger" Ephesians 6:4 says, "but bring them up in the discipline and instruction of the Lord." Similarly, 1 Corinthians 13:5 says, "love does not insist on its own way." We must understand that if we want to fix certain things in our family, we should first consider our own issues, for the blind cannot lead the blind! (Luke 6:39).

How does this all come together? *We must disciple our youth through what we teach as well as how we act.* As Christ spent three years living with his disciples, he was not only teaching them the Word of God, but he was also modeling it in obedience. The apostle Paul makes every effort to be an "example" for the church and encourages others to imitate good models so that they may grow. (1 Corinthians 11:1; 2 Thess. 3:9; Phil. 3:17) He also encourages Timothy, his spiritual student, to be an example for others despite his youth (1 Tim. 4:12).

I hope this gives us more insight into what the real purpose of a youth pastor is all about. They are another source (not the only) of mentorship, discipling, and biblical truth for the next generation. They are servants called by God to watch over the souls of people (Hebrews 13:17) – not entertainers, not baby-sitters, but men of God who genuinely do care about the spiritual growth of your youth. We as senior leadership must be willing to let them help and support them in training up the youth for the next generation. Letting them be another voice that is consistent with God's Word and teaching sends a powerful message to youth that Jesus *is* the way, the truth and the life. When we direct youth to follow these commandments, they will not only have a guide in how to live, but a purpose in living! The more we understand what is at stake when it comes to the heart of our own children, the more we will gladly take another ally who has the best spiritual intentions for our youth. I hope this encourages all senior pastors to partner with the youth pastor available, as they carry out the responsibility of spiritually leading their youth.

How Can We Better Partner With Youth Pastors?

We have made it clear that youth pastors are to be our partners, not opponents or competitors, in how we train up our youth. They are not there to entertain the children of our congregation, nor tutor them in academics, nor simply be workers in the church who are expected to do the typical church things such as retreats, lock-ins and missions trips. They are to be our brothers called by God serving with godly intentions. In Korean American churches today, we *must* shift our mentality and understanding of youth ministry from a side ministry or worse, Christian childcare, to that of a vital ministry. Youth pastors are called to be overseers of the souls of your youth (Hebrews 13:17).

As stated before, there are people who shouldn't be in the ministry, let alone be youth pastors. Although I can't cover every example, there are instances when people should not be given positions of authority. Perhaps they are the son or daughter of the senior pastor and were compelled or pressured to take the position. Another example would, people who are still trying to find their calling and purpose and end up "trying" youth ministry to see if this is where God has called them.

Ironically, one of the motivators for pursuing a partnership with youth ministry is to prevent the position from being filled by such an individual. Now that we have a good understanding of the purpose of youth ministry, what follows are some practical things to consider to help us partner with youth pastors.

Be part of the Youth Pastor Selection process

It's astounding to see the process that certain Korean churches go through in hiring their next youth pastor. It is worth investigating the recruiting process for youth pastors in our Korean churches today, and asking whether it is grounded in our cultural beliefs or grounded in scripture? Do we make the mistake of focusing on maintaining the status quo of having a youth pastor so that we can concentrate on our ministries? Do we put the spotlight on their academic aptitude and accomplishments to add an extra bullet point to our church website? What are the biggest concerns you have when taking on board a shepherd who is called to raise your church's next generation?

Occasionally, churches will actually have a solid committed process in selecting their next youth pastor. Some will even have a dedicated search committee that will interview candidates based on their calling, skillset and vision for youth ministry. Although there are many good resources that help guide this process, here is a non-exhaustive list of qualities to consider.

1. *Is he really a Christian?* This sounds obvious, but let's not assume that all pastors are good Christians. Sometimes people

who seek the ministry are very good at "doing church" but are not actually Christians (Matthew 7:21-23). Take the time to ask them for their testimony; how they came to know Christ and what their life was before and after their conversion.

2. *What was his calling into ministry?* Sometimes we automatically assume that a mature Christian is good enough to teach and lead a ministry, but this isn't always the case. God has called and gifted some, not all, to be teachers and leaders in a church (Eph. 4:11, 1 Cor. 12:1-30). Furthermore, they are to possess certain attributes and fulfill certain qualifications that confirm their calling into ministry (1 Timothy 3:1-7).

3. *What about his character?* This is something that requires time so that the candidate can prove himself and his calling. It is extremely important that any spiritual leader lives out what he teaches. We do not expect perfection, but he must be "above reproach" (1 Tim. 3:2), someone who is worth imitating (Hebrews 13:7), and one who truly seeks the best for the flock (1 Peter 5:1-11). Personal references from previous positions, his close friends, and even those he has led helps give insight into his character.

4. *Is he competent?* In the Korean culture, we tend to ask three questions when getting to know someone: What do you do? What school do you go to? What do you parents do for a living? We believe we can get a good understanding of a person by asking these questions. Unfortunately, there are times when our only standard for a good pastor is based on his degree and what school it is from. This will be a very difficult change in mentality for our Korean churches today, but there are plenty of mature Christian people qualified to lead a flock who haven't received their MDivs yet. Likewise, there are plenty people who have their doctorates but should be nowhere near the pulpit. They may know the ins-and-outs of doctrine and theology, but competence also includes empathy towards others, administration, and

an understanding of the culture. We Koreans must understand, as mentioned in earlier chapters of this text, that academics and qualifications alone do not make a good pastor. Does he have experience on the field or has he simply stayed in classrooms most of his life? Has he shown examples of going outside the box and seeking to love and serve those in the community or does it seem like he does the minimum and calls it a day?

5. *Does he have the support of the community?* Not all good pastors have to be charismatic and extroverted, but is he well-liked by the people who surround him (1 Tim. 3:7)? Do they generally feel that he has the important quality of empathy toward others? Search for someone who would actually take the time to invest in the lives of others. There are pastors whose only experience in ministry is what they've learned in school. These typically end up "going by the book" and end up having no grace towards others. Additionally, is he teachable? Does he take biblical correction well or does he seem to hide behind titles? This is not a call for perfection or for everyone to love him, but often a person who has the support of the community and is someone who possesses good traits of leadership.

Again, this is not an exhaustive list but it can offer some insight into the importance of the selection process for a youth pastor. These are not just babysitters nor are they called to simply fill a position. They are called to watch over the souls of both youth and parents. Do we not have high standards for hiring secular employees? Let us seek a biblical standard in our leaders that promotes the gospel in our churches. This will then lead us to give them the respect and honor that's due them as we seek to partner with them.

Be Involved in Youth Ministry

It greatly concerns me that parents lack initiative to meet with the youth pastor to discuss actual spiritual matters. It seems like the only time discussions happen is when their child is in trouble or when they're at their wit's end, unable to control their child.

Even though we may be busy with our personal ministry responsibilities, the youth *are* part of the body of believers. Spend time in engaging with your youth ministry. Do not let language barriers prevent you from at least saying, "hello" and "how's it going?" to your students. Ask them what they learned in church that day. Ask them what youth ministry issues you can pray for. Ask the youth pastor how you may pray for him. Knowing what they're teaching can allow you to speak the same message to your congregation about their children. Do not just be aware of the weekly meetings that your youth ministry holds, but make an effort to visit them every few months! This shows our next generation that you take spiritual matters seriously, but also shows that you want to invest into them. How do we personally, as senior leadership, show our church that Christianity goes beyond the building and the church name? How do we personally show them that our faith is an actual relationship with Christ?

One thing I appreciate about Korean congregations is their eagerness to serve with their hands. I am thankful for the numerous parents over my years in ministry who have provided great Korean food for us at retreats, offered their donations for missions, and prayed over us. Leaders, encourage parents today to be more engaged with youth ministry; to speak with one voice that our faith is more than just fulfilling weekly church obligations. Encourage parents to consider the fact that even their attendance at a youth service sends a positive message to their children. It shows our youth that they care, despite the language barrier, and shows that the faith is important to them as well.

I hope you'll notice that one of the main themes of this book is to steer away from the idea that church is simply a place to go to every week. We must show our children that these habits are byproducts of the love that we have for Christ. Even though you may not be able to understand their answers in English, ask in Korean and simply listen.

Even though you cannot pray over them in English, pray over them in Korean. Let the time of church be a time for bonding rather than a "checklist" of things to do for the week.

Do you notice that these things can only happen when *we* ourselves first love the Lord? If we have an improper mindset about the purpose of youth ministry and for that matter, Christianity, then once the honeymoon period of a new pastor dies down, things will go back to square one. When we take the time to build a relationship with them and to see their vision, that sends a message that we are one body, not a divided one. When we show our youth the biblical responses to the circumstances in life, it shows them that this is not just in the head, but a lifestyle for us. Being engaged in the youth ministry is one of the simplest steps for a good relationship with them. This leads us to our next and very important point.

Believe in Intergenerational Worship.

One unique issue with many foreign-American churches is language barrier. Usually due to the time invested in working to provide for their families, many parents simply do not have the time to attend an ESL class to strengthen their English. Fortunately some, through their own initiative and interaction with peers, are able to become literate and are able to communicate the basics with their children.

Despite learning the basics, many are still uncomfortable in English-speaking settings. Perhaps due to our Korean pride, we tend to avoid situations where we will be stumbling with our words. I feel the exact same way when I have to fumble through my poor "konglish" with native Koreans.

Consequently, you will often see many international churches in America today having segregated congregations. One for the generally older generation who are more comfortable in their native tongue, and one for those who are more comfortable with English.

Generally, in Korean churches, depending on the resources and staff available, there is a service for Korean-speaking adults,

English-speaking adults, youth, and elementary-age children. In certain churches, more groups are further broken down by age such as young adults and kindergarten. When the church is smaller in size and may not have the resources for a youth pastor, joint services where everybody participates in the main service, occasionally with a translator for the English-speaking attendees.

A question for first-generation Korean pastors: language barriers aside, what are your current thoughts on intergenerational worship and your biblical support for your response? By intergenerational worship, I mean that the congregation is not segregated by age, but all worship as one church and one body. This means that families will worship together, parents with their children, siblings with siblings, and seniors with toddlers.

Based on what has been discussed about the importance of discipleship and the close proximity required in training up our youth, which of the following worship styles would promote a better spiritual life? Segregated or intergenerational?

Do any of our personal objections towards intergenerational worship have a biblical basis? If there is no biblical hurdle, then shouldn't we work toward overcoming these obstacles rather than submitting to them?

Let's take the common language barrier issue. Will we continue to allow that to be the only reason that prevents us from reaching out to the other generation? I have witnessed very beautiful worship services where the youth are singing in English while the parents are singing in Korean. Is this not a beautiful reflection of Revelation 7:9? Despite the differences in language, they were still praising the same Lord. Practically speaking, I could offer some suggestions to encourage intergenerational worship, but this is more of an issue to be prayed over by each church, based on their current state and resources. Let us be careful that we do not make the mistake of simply putting the burden on others, expecting them to reach our standard. Make it a partnership, where the older and younger seek to speak together as one. This unity can be encouraged by simple things such as bulletins in both English and Korean, as well as lyrics for praise songs. Additionally, sermons could be divided into two sections, one English, one Korean, or if the speaker is capable, both at the same time via translation. If you do not have someone who can do this, then train someone to reach that goal. Even an effort of presenting the main points in English on screen goes a long way in showing that you care for English-speaking groups.

I've attended a fair amount of funerals in my life and I am always blessed when I hear a sermon that speaks on the hope and promise of Christ, where we will see the recently deceased again in the kingdom of heaven. It's unfortunate however to see many non-Koreans attend these services and be forced to sit through a twenty-minute sermon strictly spoken in Korean, a beautiful sermon at that! What a difference a few bullet points in English could make to a non-Korean unbeliever attending these funerals!

Case in point, these little efforts to incorporate all people within the worship service goes very far in the discipling of our children, and the non-Koreans who will enter our church doors someday. In the kingdom of heaven, we *will* be worshipping the Lord not in separate rooms or service times, but together, and that includes all of our children as well!

There are many blessings when a family hears a sermon together and feels the encouragement, counsel, redirection and conviction of hearing God's Word together. Perhaps a family has been arguing over something and they hear the importance of forgiving each other seventy times seven (Matthew 18:22), or even teachings on honoring your parents and fathers doing their best to model Christ to their youth (Ephesians 6:1-4).

Consider these things compared to the possible effects of segregated worship services. Human nature is funny. As D.A. Carson, a famous Christian theologian, once said, we don't "drift into holiness." Instead when we get used to comfort, we become complacent, and once we become complacent, we begin to compromise. It *is* easier to drop off your children at the elementary or youth ministries on Sunday because you need a break from them. It allows you to catch your breath, while you let the youth pastor handle the rest. When we experience the positives that come from the easier choice, we will slowly drift into trusting it more and more, gradually taking it for granted and eventually letting others take over the responsibility of raising our children.

Christ himself warned against this mentality in Matthew 7:13-14, as he speaks for true believers to "enter through the narrow gate, for the wide and broad entrance leads to destruction." We should aim to promote an environment and culture in our church today where it's not simply a "checklist" of things to do for the week, but one that truly seeks the kingdom of God in all things. This means to work together with other parents, with your pastoral leadership team (especially the youth pastor), and to be the body of Christ carrying out the Great commission handed over to us.

Some of you may be asking, if we are to seek a culture where parents lead their children spiritually, does this mean that we should get rid of youth pastors as a whole? Some churches have chosen to have a "family pastor" as opposed to a youth pastor to fight the stigma that the spiritual care of the youth is the responsibility of the local church. This is fine, but we need to be careful that we do not allow our church to be led by generalizations, but that we consider the calling the Lord has given to us. As a former youth pastor myself, I believe that pastors should work so as to eventually no longer be needed.

When I consider the apostle Paul and his passion for planting churches in Asia Minor, it's hard to deny the fact that he had a solid discipleship vision for ministry. He understood that it was about Christ first, not himself (1 Cor. 1:10-17), and that due to the nature of his calling he could pass from this earth at any moment (Phil. 1:21). Therefore, it was imperative that he raise up leaders such as Timothy and Titus.

I am not endorsing a structure where youth pastors have a limited period of time before they are transferred to another church, as some denominations practice. It is understood that if we are to first seek the kingdom of God, carry out the Great Commission, and bring glory to the Lord and not man, we should have a vision that seeks to expand the kingdom instead of simply becoming comfortable with our current church.

In fact, to be even more specific, I am speaking about church planting. When a church has grown to a significant number and has enough solid leaders and gifted people, they should begin a new church in another area of need with the same discipleship-oriented vision. Can you imagine a youth pastor who has trained enough leaders for a certain number of years at one church; leaders who are capable of directing the youth ministry so that this youth pastor is able to plant a church elsewhere and repeat the process? To have that desire is to first seek the kingdom of God and not ours![25]

I hope that we see the contrast between a church or ministry that first seeks to worship and glorify God, compared to one where we simply fall back to the cultural traditions we have been brought up with. If we are being honest with ourselves in truly seeking a Christ-centered youth ministry, then I pray that we will promote an environment where we partner with those who love the next generation. We will never achieve this if we still secretly desire "well-behaved, high-achieving Korean children." No change means a continued culture of rebellion, that we will continue to lose our children spiritually, and the eventual closing of our church doors.

What do we personally do to show our congregation and youth that our faith is not about fulfilling obligations, but showing an actual adoration for the Lord? That sends a powerful message to them that the Lord is real and alive. A discipleship culture shows that Christianity is not a cultural thing, but that it is a spiritual matter, a matter that deals with mankind as a whole, and our relationship with our Creator and our Savior.

---

[25] Derek Seipp has written an excellent book, *Innovation in World Mission*, concerning how churches can work toward adapting to the everchanging cultures throughout history. ISBN-10: 0878083979

Therefore do not be anxious, saying, 'What shall we eat?' or 'What shall we drink?' or 'What shall we wear?' For the Gentiles seek after all these things, and your heavenly Father knows that you need them all. But seek first the kingdom of God and his righteousness, and all these things will be added to you. Therefore do not be anxious about tomorrow, for tomorrow will be anxious for itself. Sufficient for the day is its own trouble. – Matthew 6:31-34

CHAPTER 11
Encouragement for 2nd & 3rd Generation Pastors

To my dear brothers and sisters in ministry,

It is worth it.

Ministry, with all the hardships, pain, and frustration is still worth it.

Even when it feels like you'll never see the fruit of your labors, or that the entire church is against you, or that you have those days where you doubt your calling, please be encouraged that it is still worth it.

I wrote this book with ten humbling years of ministry behind me that consisted more of hardships than joys. You would think I would never want to touch anything ministry-oriented ever again, especially after being in an environment that seemingly is so anti-gospel sometimes, but, yes, it is still worth it.

Christ is worth it, and he deserves the glory. Tribulation is something that more clearly shows us what it means when Paul says, "to live is Christ and to die is gain" (Philippians 1:21). Our Lord was so correct in more ways than one when he taught us to pray for more workers because the harvest is so plentiful. May you do whatever it takes to stand firm in your faith and in your calling, continuing to deny yourself and carry your cross to follow Him.

In this chapter, I would like to offer some practical advice and encouragement for anyone who is considering fulfilling their calling in serving the Korean American church.

Choose Your Church Carefully – "Shepherd the flock of God that is among you, exercising oversight, not under compulsion, but willingly as God would have you" (1 Peter 5:2). Peter encourages elders to consider both their motives and methods as they fulfill their calling. Sometimes in the pursuit of getting involved in ministry, new pastors can eagerly accept any calling without really assessing and praying over some important factors. As Paul gives a great analogy of how marriage is like Christ's relationship to the church, it would be wise for us to ask certain questions before we "marry" a church. Even though it may seem that the church has many external redeeming qualities, it is wise to take the time to probe more deeply into certain issues that will affect the way that you carry out your ministry. Consider the following questions:

- *Will I be expected to lead on my own, or will I report to someone?*
- *Will they disciple me in the process or will I be expected to have the skills already?*
- *How does this church deal with conflict resolution and discipline?*
- *What is their ministry philosophy and what are some examples of them putting this vision into action?*
- *Will this church take good care of my family?*
- *How will this church help me in my weaknesses?*
- *How will we work out any major or minor doctrinal disagreements?*

- *Will my gifts further or hinder the church's current vision and execution?*
- *Why did the previous pastor leave? (If applicable)*

As with many new things, there is always the honeymoon period where it seems as if nothing can go wrong, but the real test of ministry is when something does go wrong and you examine how the church responds to it. Let your decision be influenced mainly by what the Lord has called you to and gifted to you, and whether or not the church recognizes those things and wants to partner with you.

Learn Korean – As time passes, this is becoming less of an issue with more and more second and third-generation families become the majority within Korean churches today. There is still a huge need, however, to communicate clearly with leadership and with families about your ministry goals and expectations. Although many may speak English today, cultural idioms and slang can impact how well leadership communicates with you. If possible, do your best to learn the language so that it is another skill that you can use to bless others, rather than a hurdle that you must overcome.

Create a contract – This may seem offensive to some, but let us not deny the fact that Koreans do not uphold a written contract-oriented culture. In an honor-shame society, our words are just as good as a contract, as the one who is not true to their word can be viewed as an outcast by the community. The fear of a ruined reputation is a great deterrent to breaching an agreement. However, for your sake, it is highly encouraged that you have your contract written on paper, not just for your protection, but for clarity regarding expectations and responsibilities. Also, make sure that your contract is clear concerning sabbaticals and be certain that the church is willing to uphold the agreement. It comes down to this: a church that puts in the effort of creating a contract that is clear on responsibilities and how the pastor is to be is a church that probably does well in taking care of their pastors. A church that is not willing to do so reveals what they actually think about the position.

Communicate with your senior leadership as much as possible – As difficult as it may be at times, it is beneficial to have open dialogue with your pastors as frequently as possible. This may require more grace on our end as second and third-generation Korean Americans, as there will be first-generation expectations placed upon us. Let us offer grace and understanding by being patient, but also realize that even our senior pastors have grown up in a certain culture which has molded their current worldviews. Consider people like Joseph and Daniel who grew up in foreign lands, but because of their integrity, were entrusted with power and responsibility from *foreign leaders.* 1 Timothy 4:12 encourages us not to let anybody despise us for our youth. We are to set an example by our speech and conduct. Not all pastors will be as open to this communication at first, but let us be faithful to our calling and trust that the Lord will judge accordingly.

Youth pastors, partner with parents as much as possible – It's quite simple, but you want your parents to be your allies rather than your opponents. The earlier you set the tone that you want to work alongside them in spiritually training their children, the easier this becomes. Depending on the current spiritual temperature of your church, the method and the amount of time you will need to build up these relationships will vary. I have found through my experience that when you actually put in the time and effort to invest in a relationship, showing that you do care for the wellbeing of a student, parents will take notice and appreciate it. Simple things such as calling them, spending time with them, and any disciple-oriented ministry model will definitely plant seeds of trust in the parents, showing that you care. In a Korean context where confrontation is mostly avoided, do your best to settle conflict and disagreements in person as soon as possible. Stand firm in your convictions and ministry when parents complain about the lack of "events" or "fun things" in church, for it is better for you to be hated for living out the truth of Christ, rather than preaching things that tickle the ears of people. As difficult as it may be, your steadfastness in biblical truth plants seeds into their hearts. You may never know, but perhaps as the Lord works in them, they too will see the blessings that come from your focus on the Gospel. Invite them to services and projects as much as possible. Do not be content in segregated youth programs but get parents involved as much as possible with even just monthly newsletters. This is where being fluent in Korean becomes a blessing!

Have an accountability group that will pray for you – As with any leadership or ministry position, it is a multi-person job. Especially for those who currently serve in an environment where they lack a mentor or plurality of elders who can teach and hold them accountable. Even in this situation, we are not excused from being accountable to someone. Find close friends, take efforts to find networking for youth pastors in the area, and do what it takes to get that encouragement from other voices who are probably going through the same hardships as you. Sometimes your spouse can be a great place to express your frustrations, but I also encourage having others to be extra ears and shoulders to lean upon.

To be honest, I wish there was a way that I could go out and hug every second-generation pastor, who through the hardships and frustrations struggle with whether or not they should continue their ministry. Know that instead of looking for a generalized answer for your current situation, you should pray often. The voice of the Lord is the first voice you should always seek. To follow and obey that voice will be fearful because of the potential changes and hardship that may come, but the Lord has proven again and again his faithfulness. In your own life, may you trust and believe the words that you preach every Sunday and may that help guide you in making godly decisions.

CHAPTER 12
The Biblical Reason for Education

Speaking as a Korean who grew up under high academic expectations, the concept of education has always been close to my heart. I've had the privilege of teaching in private schools for about 5 years in a variety of subjects and so I've had the pleasure of experiencing all the things that come with teaching. By the way, any teachers who are reading this right now: God bless you. I know how difficult things are and I know how increasingly difficult things are becoming when it comes to simply doing your passion: to teach!

With such a high emphasis on academics in the Korean community, I want to share some guidelines and give direction concerning the biblical purpose for why we learn. One of the biggest reasons why we have so many issues within the education system today is because the hearts of so many students (as well as their parents) have forgotten the true purpose of what learning is all about! We can shove all the money, technology, and new things into schools all we want, but if the hearts of the people do not understand why they learn, it doesn't matter how many tools we have.

I can summarize the answer in two statements. The purpose of learning is 1) to discover more of God, his character and attributes so that we may appreciate and glorify him more, and 2) to gain skills and knowledge so that we can love our neighbors better.

Does this sound familiar? These are the two greatest commandments that our Lord gave to us in Matthew 22:37-40. You must first love the Lord with all your heart, all your soul, and all your **mind**. I believe Jesus was being both literal and figurative here. We *are* to give the Lord everything that we have, and we are called to love him sacrificially (Romans 12:1), and that includes our minds! Therefore, the purpose of learning is transformed from being a mere achievement. It becomes more than just working for that degree and recognition from people and perhaps the money and influence we gain from it. It no longer becomes something to gain from the world, but rather education becomes an *act of worship*.

Let me offer some examples of what happens when we actively learn this belief:

Math and Science: Math is no longer about memorizing formulas and postulates. It is no longer about simply "finding x" and making sure each equation is balanced, but now you're learning about how God used math to create this universe. The basis of all natural sciences comes down to mathematical truth. Biology is based in chemistry, chemistry is based in physics, and physics is based in math. As one of my close peers told me, "Math is the language that God used to create creation." All the concepts and patterns of life, such as the environment, our own bodies, the solar systems, and so on are written with design which can be explained mathematically! The subject of math is discovering the patterns that God has created to show his creation!

English: I'll be honest with you. I never had a great experience in my English classes throughout high school and college. I never liked the books that we had to read, never loved learning vocabulary, or the rules of grammar and syntax. English without the presence of God is simply another tool that we use for success.

Let's put God back into the picture concerning English. Vocabulary and grammar are now about seeking clarity in communication, especially when expressing the love of Christ towards others and the truth of God's Word. Literature is no longer about simply reading the old stories of dead men of the past, but a study into the minds and hearts of people and their struggles with life. What if we viewed fiction as attempts to describe the state of mankind's condition in this world? Studying these texts can actually show the need for biblical truth and for Christ! The better we are at articulating ourselves, the more efficiently we're able to describe the majesties of Christ and the truths behind our faith!

History: Another subject that I had absolutely no connection with as a student. Dates? Wars? Major events that happened in the past? These are things that many high school students have no interest in, but when we understand that history is observing the patterns of behavior, struggle, and sinfulness of men throughout time, and how it points to our need for a Savior, then look no further than your history class. Not only that, the more you know about the past, the more you'll also notice the sovereignty of God.

Civics: Want to really see the depravity of men and their hearts? Study different governments and the need for laws and regulations and see how often laws cannot do what they were meant to do.

Music: See how well music is organized and designed? See how that reflects our God who created? Take the time to see the parallels between music and math and discover how beautiful our Creator is!

Languages: Do you realize the need for sharing the gospel today? In different languages? In different cultures?

I could go on and on, but I hope this gives you some insight and encouragement about the real purpose of studying. When we toil for worldly temporary things, the required work becomes tedious, lifeless and without purpose. When the cause is for something eternal, we may find ourselves even learning random subjects to simply discover more about our God and how we can love others!

My encouragement to students who have rigid parents with high academic standards: simply do your best. First, do it for the Lord and then secondly to honor your parents. Remind yourself continuously of the godly reason for learning. Seek, ask questions, hold discussions with your pastor and other mature believers about what the purpose of a certain subject is and how it can be applied biblically today. The more you learn to love how to learn, the less lecturing and pressure there will be from your parents to do well in school!

Concluding Thoughts

It is my prayer that this book has provoked thought, offered encouragement to those who have a continued passion for the Korean American community, and point people to a Christ-driven lifestyle and church culture. I pray that our identities are always grounded first in Christ, that our work is always gospel-centered, and that our priorities are first seeking his kingdom. At the end of it all, many nations and tribes will be professing with their lips that Jesus Christ is Lord! May our highest regard always be his Word alone led by the Spirit alone. I am blessed to be called a Korean American. Despite the hardships I would never give up my status as a Korean growing up in the US. But my ultimate source of value and purpose come from Christ first. May He be the reason why you continue in your ministries, love difficult parents, and work toward bringing people to the life-giving Gospel.

> *"Jesus said to him, 'I am the way, and the truth, and the life. No one comes to the Father except through me.'"*
> *– John 14:6*

Special Thanks

There is an old African proverb that says, "It takes a village to raise a child." The same could be said about writing a book. This text could not have been possible without the support and help from many of my peers and loved ones. Thanks to all of those who showed interest and encouraged me throughout this entire process, but especially to a select few:

- ✦ Rose Chang and Micah Chung for helping with the design of the book cover!
- ✦ Young shin Chun, Sheela Yi, Barbara Pyles, Gloria Pak, and especially David Getz for proofreading, editing, and correcting my numerous mistakes.
- ✦ Advancing Native Missions for being an amazing organization of brothers and sisters tirelessly working for the kingdom of God. Check them out at www.AdvancingNativeMissions.com!
- ✦ To the numerous brothers and sisters that I have met over the years, challenging me to grow beyond a complacent Christian faith, and listening to me rant about the Korean American Church.

The Ministry of ANM

*ANM Publications is a ministry initiative of
Advancing Native Missions*

Advancing Native Missions (ANM) is a U.S.-based Christian missions agency. However, unlike many such agencies that are involved in sending missionaries from America to other places around the world, ANM works with indigenous missionaries. Indigenous (or native) missionaries are Christian workers who minister within their own sphere of influence proclaiming the Gospel of Jesus Christ to their own people. ANM then works to connect Christians in America with these brothers and sisters, to equip and encourage them. Our goal is to build relationships of love and trust between indigenous missionaries and North American individuals and churches. In this way, the entire body of Christ becomes involved in completing the Great Commission. *"And this gospel of the kingdom shall be preached in all the world as a witness to all nations, and then the end shall come"* (Matthew 24:14).

If you would like to know how you can become an effective coworker with native missionaries to reach the unreached for Jesus Christ, contact ANM at contact@AdvancingNativeMissions.com, call us at 540-456-7111, or visit our website: www.AdvancingNative Missions.com.

CPSIA information can be obtained
at www.ICGtesting.com
Printed in the USA
BVHW071942090622
639355BV00004B/18